CLOWN SKITS
FOR EVERYONE

by Happy Jack Feder

illustrations by
Lafe Locke

D0868926

MERIWETHER PUBLISHING LTD.
Colorado Springs, Colorado

Meriwether Publishing Ltd., Publisher
Box 7710
Colorado Springs, CO 80933

Editor: Arthur L. Zapel
Typesetting: Sharon Garlock and Leah Speckhals
Cover design and illustrations: Lafe Locke
Art direction: Tom Myers

© Copyright MCMXCI Meriwether Publishing Ltd.
Printed in the United States of America
Second Edition

Library of Congress Cataloging-in-Publication Data

Feder, Happy Jack.
    Clown skits for everyone / Happy Jack Feder. -- 2nd ed. /
illustrated by Lafe Locke.
        p.   cm.
    Summary: A collection of thirty-two clown skits for one or two performers, accompanied by tips for aspiring clowns on props, gestures, terminology, and safety.
    ISBN 0-916260-75-5 : $9.95
    1. Clowns. 2. Amateur plays. [1. Clowns. 2. Plays.]
PN1955.F43   1991
812'.54--dc20   90-29297
                                                  CIP
                                                  AC

To the memory of
Toby T. Twist,
the world's greatest clown, entrepreneur,
teacher, and friend,
who had more going for him
than he ever knew

Contents

SILLY SOLOS

DIZZY DUETS

Clown Skits for Everyone (and That Means Everyone!)

This book is a handy aid for anyone and everyone who is ever in need of clown performance material or bits of advice on *how* to perform. Not only professional clowns will be interested in *Clown Skits for Everyone,* but so will teachers, students, talent show participants, members of fraternal and social organizations, and people who'd just like to give the practice of clowning around a quick whirl.

This book contains dozens of fully scripted skits designed to be used by one or two clowns. Each skit is quickly learned, simple to prepare for, and — most important — guaranteed to bring big laughs and roaring rounds of applause. No one, not even the amateur clown who gets stuck doing a clown show for his or her club's annual charity banquet, need worry about putting on a fine performance — not if they use this book!

So let's join up with our hosts, Merry Melody and Smiling Sam, and let them show us some great skits. Every now and then, Merry Melody will take a break and offer us her *Musings,* and Smiling Sam his *Secrets:* advice and observations on being a good clown.

Off we go!

The Road to Clowntown

One day, when the sun was way up high in the sky, and the little birds were singing pretty songs, and the trees were green, and the flowers bright, Smiling Sam, a part-time clown, decided to venture into the happy village of Clowntown.

"Hi-de-ho, and away we go!" sang Smiling Sam, who, with a hop and a skip, began sauntering down the lane. So excited and enthusiastic was he about his travels, he didn't even notice that he bumped into, knocked flat, and walked over, one Mary McBlurp, a woman who had little time for foolishness.

"Hey!" cried Mary McBlurp, "Hey you! Smiling Sam! That hurt. Now get back here and help me up."

Smiling Sam soon realized what he had done and apologized profusely.

"Gosh, I'm really sorry. I didn't intend to hurt you. It's just that, well, I was on my way to Clowntown, you see, and —"

"Clowntown!" snorted Mary McBlurp. "What a silly name!"

Smiling Sam agreed. "That's because it's a silly place. Only fun things happen there. In Clowntown, for instance, you wouldn't actually feel pain if I were to walk over you. You would just pretend to be hurt."

Mary McBlurp, who had regained her composure, found herself expressing a mild interest (while harboring a deeper one).

"And why would I pretend to such a thing?"

"To entertain the children, that's why! Children everywhere — those in China and New Jersey, the North Pole and Detroit, along with the children still tucked away inside grampas and mamas and bankers and bakers — need to be entertained by people like us. Clowns!"

Try as she might, Mary McBlurp couldn't help but smile. She was a lot like you and me, in that even though she had no time for foolishness, she wished she did.

"What are you talking about, eh, Smiling Sam? I'm no clown."

1

"Oh, but I bet you are! Or that you could be!"

Poor Mary McBlurp sighed as her smile vanished and shoulders drooped. "I don't think I could ever be a clown. I don't know how to make people laugh. I — oh! I think Clowntown is a silly name." Mary McBlurp scowled.

"It is."

"For a silly place."

"That's true."

"For silly people."

"No argument there. You know what I think?"

She looked up at him and pursed her lips in mild defiance. "What?"

"I think that even though you pretend not to, you'd like to clown around. You'd feel right at home in Clowntown. It's your kind of town."

Mary McBlurp's eyes dazzled as she cried with glee. "Do you think? Oh, yes! Secretly (how did you know?) I've always wanted to be a clown. Doesn't everyone? But my problem, Smiling Sam, is that I don't know how to be a clown. I'm afraid I'd be lost in Clowntown. I wouldn't know what to do, how to act, or where to go."

"Ah, but not if I were to serve as your tour guide! What do you say?" Smiling Sam held out one arm for her to take, and gestured toward the lane with the other. Still, she hesitated.

"Do you honestly think I could be a clown in Clowntown?"

"Why not? You already have the most important qualification: *desire!* And with me to show you the ropes, you won't have a problem in the world. I'll teach you everything you need to know."

Mary McBlurp tightened her belt, gritted her teeth, and took Smiling Sam's arm. "What have I got to lose?"

"That's the spirit!"

Off they went down the lane, bound for Clowntown. They were laughing and singing when they began, but, hours later, still searching for Clowntown, they began to frown.

"What's up?" asked Mary McBlurp. "Are we lost?"

Smiling Sam scratched his head. "I don't think so. I've never had any problems finding it before. Just find an audience — families in pizza or ice cream parlors, kids at birthday parties, people watching parades or attending grand opening sales at stores, even banqueteers at get-togethers — and you've found Clowntown. But so far we've had bad — HEY! Got an idea! Your name!"

"What about it?"

"Change it from a people name to a clown name, and maybe we'll find Clowntown. Mary McBlurp is OK, but a clown should have a special, happy —"

"Merry Melody?"

"Wonderful! *Merry Melody.* I like that. With a name like that, we'll be in Clowntown in no time."

And again they waltzed down the lane, and again they didn't find Clowntown.

"I just can't figure this out," said Smiling Sam. "I've never had any problems — HEY! Got another idea! Maybe if we start talking like . . .

Smiling Sam: . . . this, we'll be able to walk right in. I'm sure it'll work. *(MERRY MELODY shook her head. "What's the dif', anyway?")* There's a big difference. When we talk like this, it's a lot easier for the audience (and each of us) to understand what we're saying. All clowns in Clowntown talk like this.

Merry Melody: Who am I to argue?

Smiling Sam: And if we should ever manage to clamp our yaps long enough to actually do something, we not only do it in the present tense, but we do it in italics, to boot! *(To illustrate his point, SMILING SAM kicks himself in the hindquarters and turns a somersault. MERRY MELODY claps her hands and laughs.)*

Merry Melody: This is going to be more fun than I thought. Let's hurry! Clowntown or bust!

Smiling Sam: Clowntown or Frowntown, you mean! *(They don't bust or end up in Frowntown, but they don't find Clowntown, either. Their spirits are at a low ebb.)*

3

Merry Melody: Don't feel bad, Smiling Sam. I'm sure it's my fault that we can't find Clowntown. I'm afraid I'm not a real clown. You go on without me and —

Smiling Sam: That's it! You hit the head on the nail! Just look at yourself!

Merry Melody: Watch it, buster. I'm a perfectly normal person. There's nothing wrong with me.

Smiling Sam: Precisely. We've got to make you look perfectly abnormal, like me. You need a bright, colorful face with big orange eyes and purple circles and a giant red smile, not to mention whacky clothes and whatnot. You need to look like a clown. Let's get started!

Here's what Merry Melody will be working with: a make-up brush; a jar of whiteface; different colors of grease paint; a black eyeliner pencil; and a red foam rubber nose applied with spirit gum.

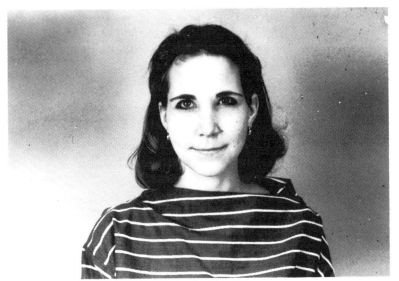

And here's Merry Melody, confounded and consternated as to how in the heck she's ever going to look like a clown! But with her hair pulled back and her face squeaky clean, she's ready to try anything.

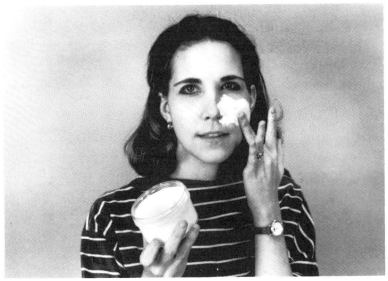

She takes the plunge and starts smearing the whiteface over her cheeks. Notice how clever she is in using only one finger, keeping the others clean. She spreads the goop on evenly, and not too heavily.

YIKES! She looks like a ghost from the grave, doesn't she? She's plastered white from ear to ear, although it fades away toward the bottom of her neck.

Eye ay ay! She's putting the finishing touches of orange grease paint on her eyes. Like all smart clowns, she knows the eyes are the critical part of the clown face and should be applied first. Every other detail should be built out from the eyes.

With a bit of red grease paint, Merry Melody slaps on a smile! Well, almost *a smile.*

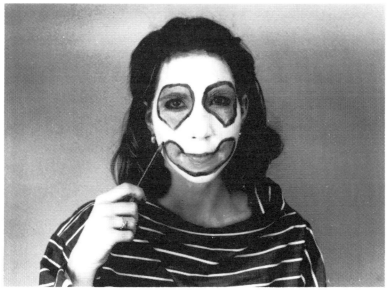

Not quite satisfied, she outlines her eyes, mouth, and entire face with a black eyeliner pencil. This does a lot to help the colors stand out as well as to give strong clarity to the shapes.

Surprise! See what a little big ol' clown nose can do for a clown?

Top it all off with a funny hat, a curly wig, suspenders, baggy pants with patches, brightly colored shirts and scarves, and you've got yourself one real live clown!

Smiling Sam: My, my! You are one smart looking clown, Merry Melody, if ever there was a dumb one.

Merry Melody: Are we finally ready for Clowntown?

Smiling Sam: You bet. But is Clowntown ready for us?

SILLY SOLOS

Merry Melody and Smiling Sam no sooner enter Clowntown than they get caught in a clown stampede and become separated. Merry Melody isn't worried, though, for she quickly finds an audience. Once in front of a crowd, the jokes and pranks fly faster than she imagined possible. . . .

The Exploding Balloon

Props: A large round balloon, a thumbtack, and a rubber snake.

Comments: Lucky for Merry Melody that she's starting out with a simple routine that never fails to get an audience roused up. This is a good opener for beginning and experienced clowns alike.

• • • • •

(MERRY MELODY stands in front of her audience, smugly tugging on her suspenders.)

Merry Melody: Hello, boys and girls! Say, have I ever got a surprise for you! When I found out I was coming to your party, I went to the store and bought the biggest, largest, most humongous, mostest giganticust balloon in the whole, entire world! Why, this balloon is even bigger than my whole refrigerator! Would you like to see my balloon? *(The children in the audience nod yes. MERRY MELODY smiles and digs into her pockets for the — uh oh! No balloon! She can't find it in any of her pockets!)*

Whoopsa doopsy! Merry Melody got out of the wrong side of the tree this morning, boys and girls. Aw, but you didn't really want to see the world's biggest balloon anyway, did you? *(Some of the children answer that they indeed do want to see the balloon. MERRY MELODY can't seem to hear them, though. She squints her face and leans forward.)* What's that? I can't hear you. *(This time the children answer louder, hurting MERRY MELODY's eardrums. The excitement is beginning to build.)* Ouch! OK, I guess I'd better find it. Now . . . I wonder where it is? *(Again she searches her pockets. What's that? Could it be the balloon? She smiles, pulls out a — snake! Fortunately, it's only made of rubber.)*

That scared me! I didn't expect to find a snake in

that pocket. I always keep my snakes in the other pocket. *(MERRY MELODY continues searching. She pulls off a shoe, shakes it, and EUREKA! the balloon drops out. Secretly, she also pulls a thumbtack out of the sole of the shoe. Replacing the shoe, she holds up a rather crumpled, flattened balloon.)* Here's the balloon, but — it's all tiny! It's even tinier than an old horn! What do you think I should do to make it real big again? *(The children tell her to blow it up. Somewhat confused, MERRY MELODY holds the balloon in her fingers, a few inches away from her mouth, and blows at it.)*

Children: No, no! Blow it UP! Put it in your mouth and blow it up!

Merry Melody: *(Aghast)* In my MOUTH?!

Children: Yes! Yes! Blow it up!

Merry Melody: If you think that will make it bigger than my whole refrigerator and not as small as an old horn, I'll give it a try. *(MERRY MELODY shrugs, tilts her head back, puts the entire balloon in her mouth, and promptly blows, spitting it above her head. The children, frustrated and giggling, again give the clown simple instructions. MERRY MELODY appears to understand.)* Oh! You mean put it BETWEEN my lips and blow! You should have said so in the first place! *(She does as instructed, but removes her hands. She blows the balloon out of her mouth and onto the floor. This time the children tell her to hold the balloon while blowing.)* OK, I'll try it. But you'd better be right this time, or I'm going to take this balloon back to the store and demand customer satisfaction, and in all colors, too! *(MERRY MELODY finally does everything correctly. She takes a big, deep breath and blows once into the balloon. It inflates only a little bit. MERRY MELODY scratches her head.)*

I don't know . . . when I bought this balloon, they said it would be bigger than my whole entire refrigerator. But it isn't. What am I going to do? *(The children yell for her to blow it bigger. She takes another*

deep breath and blows again. The balloon grows.)
Bigger?

Children: Yes! Bigger! Bigger! *(Each time MERRY MELODY inflates the balloon, she pauses to ask if she should continue. Each time the children answer yes with louder and louder voices. Faces are scrunched tight with anticipation of the explosion of the growing balloon. No matter what MERRY MELODY says, no one really believes the balloon will grow bigger than a refrigerator — not even MERRY MELODY. That's why she secretly pokes it with the thumbtack [after dragging out every last bit of suspense]. The children shriek and laugh.)* We sure got a bang out of that, didn't we? Even if the balloon wasn't as big as my entire refrigerator!

Pool Ball Prankster

Props: Pool cue, wire coat hanger, three pool balls.

Comments: It was only natural that Smiling Sam (who spends more time in pool halls than one might imagine) should invent this routine. If you'd like to perform it without performing the same pool hall research that Smiling Sam did, just read the following instructions:

Cut a twelve-inch length of wire from the coat hanger and straighten it. Bend a half-inch tab at the end.

Drill a hole through the center of each of the pool balls that allows the wire to slide through easily (but without wobble).

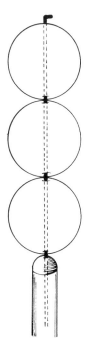

Cut an eight- to ten-inch slit (as wide as the hole in the balls) in the thick end of the cue. The cut shouldn't extend beyond the center of the cue's diameter. For best results, use a table saw.

Stick the wire in the slot, and jam in a few chips of wood to hold it in place. You're finished!

What? Don't know what to do with it? Let Smiling Sam show you.

• • • • •

(On the other side of Clowntown, the children in another audience watch SMILING SAM very closely while he makes strange faces and digs deep into his pockets.)

Smiling Sam: What the . . . ? I've got some things in my pockets and I don't know what they are, or what they're trying to do, but . . . but I guess we'd better find out, OK? *(The children agree, and SMILING SAM pulls the pool balls out of his pockets.)* Look at that! Pool balls! Three pool balls! And they were in my pockets! What's the world coming to, anyway? *(Pause, no answer)* Well, I don't know what it's coming to either, so I guess we're even. But! I do know one thing! I've got to do something *special* with these pool balls. I know! I'll juggle them. How about that? *(He tosses the balls in the air and promptly drops them on the floor.)* Oops! So much for juggling. *(SMILING SAM picks up the balls and then reaches for his pool cue.)*

How about a game of pool, huh? Hold on, I'm just kidding. I don't even have a pool table! I guess that leaves me no choice but to . . . BALANCE! Balance all three of these balls on the very, absolute, definitively defined end of this pool cue. You kids will have to help me, though, because this balancing trick is probably about the hardest trick in the world. Here's what I want you to do: Every time I touch my finger to my nose, yell SUCKERS so loud that even these pool balls can hear you. All right? *(SMILING SAM quickly touches his finger to his nose, and the children yell.)* Ha! That's not so loud. You've got to yell louder than that for these pool balls to hear you. One more time. *(He slowly brings his finger to his nose, allowing anticipation and energy to build. It works every time.)* That's what I like to hear. Now we can move on to some serious balancing.

(SMILING SAM's smile vanishes as he carefully holds the cue up, with the slit at the top, facing him and out of view of the audience. He prepares to place a ball on the end of the cue and, for some aid, touches his nose. This is where SMILING SAM gets sneaky. After finding the almost invisible hole in the ball, he pushes up on the wire, sliding it into the ball. No one notices. He removes his hand — voilà! A balanced ball!)

So far, so great! Now . . . *(He puts the bottom of the cue in the palm of his hand and makes a simple balancing act look easy.)* Now for two! *(He carefully repeats the legerdemain with a second ball. Again he touches his nose for a deafening roar of SUCKERS. He's now balancing one ball on top of another ball on top of a cue. At least, that's what everyone thinks. One troublesome boy thinks otherwise.)*

Troublesome Boy: Hey! You're not really balancing those balls, you're sticking — *(This has happened more than once to SMILING SAM, so he knows what to do. He quickly grabs the two balls, holds them in position, and rushes to the boy to whisper in his ear.)*

Smiling Sam: Hold the noise! Keep quiet and I'll let you help me in the rest of the show, OK? It'll be our secret. *(How can the boy refuse such a wonderful offer? SMIL-ING SAM goes back to balancing.)* Time now for THREE BALLS! *(He takes the last ball and very carefully lowers the cue, so that the balanced balls are in front of his nose. The tension is high and he shakes. He slowly sets the third ball on top of the second and pulls his hand away. He pretends to have difficulty balancing the balls and touches his finger to his nose for a helpful shout of SUCKERS. He again balances the cue in the palm of his hand.)*

Three balls! One ball on top of another ball on top of — can you believe it — another ball, on top of a cue stick, on top of my hand! Where, oh, where is my applause? *(Everyone applauds.)* That's better. Now for the grand opening — er, I mean, the grand ending! *(He touches his finger to his nose.)*

Children: SUCKERS! SUCKERS!

Smiling Sam: Louder!

Children: SUCKERS! SUCKERS!

Smiling Sam: Suckers! I'll say you're suckers! *(To everyone's surprise, he lets the cue hang over his shoulders at about a forty-five degree angle. The balls, held by the wire, are still in place! The audience realizes it's been duped and groans, causing SMILING SAM to laugh louder. He puts the cue away, being careful not to reveal the secret of the trick.)*

MERRY
MELODY'S
MUSINGS

Gestures and Actions

The first time I performed in front of an audience, I was a nervous wreck! Honest! I ran around like a chicken with its head cut off, hoping that if I moved fast enough, no one would see that I was a beginner. *Well!* I didn't fool anyone. In fact, I made everyone else at least half as nervous as I was, because they could see I wasn't relaxed.

Do you want to know what I learned the hard way? Move slow and steady. Control your actions. Make every movement purposeful! When you're all decked out in your clown uniform, you're one big eyeful for those little kids (who can be easily confused). So keep your actions simple, smooth, and relaxed. Clowns aren't cartoon characters inside the safe television box; they're big and real and complex and even a little threatening to some kids. Everything you can do to add comfort and simplicity to the performance is a plus in your favor. This includes facial gestures, which should also be very big and very simple. If you develop expressions for happiness, sorrow, anger, and confusion, you'll cover the entire spectrum of clown emotions.

Remember: Keep actions and gestures big to see and simple to understand!

Unbalancing Water Balloons

Props: A dozen small round balloons, two filled with water, two filled with air, and a large pan or shallow bucket which can be firmly and *safely* attached (you don't want it to fall off!) to the end of a pool cue.

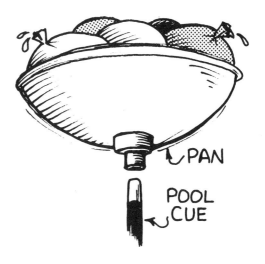

PAN

POOL
CUE

Comments: Smiling Sam isn't the only one who can balance things. In this routine, Merry Melody balances a pole holding a tray of water (so they think!) balloons. In the process, she also unbalances a few minds.

• • • • •

(MERRY MELODY rubs her hands together, stands on her toes, and smiles with glee.)

Merry Melody: Hey, guys! Listen carefully, because Merry Melody has something special to tell you! Are you listening? *(Pauses while children nod.)* Good. Now, when you look at me, what do you see? What am I? Who am I?

Children: A clown! You're Merry Melody the Clown!

Merry Melody: That's darn right! But I'm also something

more than a clown. Something more than Merry
Melody. I'm also the world's greatest balancer of things!
Why, I can balance a fat elephant on my left knee and
you'll say GEE! I can balance a broken lawnmower on
a cow and you'll say WOW! Or cold mashed potatoes
on a plate and you'll all say GREAT! I can balance all
those things — but I won't! Nope. Not today. I'm not
going to balance a fat elephant or a broken lawnmower
or cold mashed potatoes because I ... I ... *(Embar-
rased)* I didn't bring them with me. Instead, I brought ...
REAL   LIVE   WATER   BALLOONS!   *(MERRY
MELODY pulls a water balloon out of her pan, grins
from ear to ear, and tosses the balloon from hand to
hand. Some of the children, especially those nearest to
MERRY MELODY [and the water balloon], become
giggly and nervous. MERRY MELODY steps back.)*
You're not worried that I'm going to drop a real live
water balloon on you, are you? You are? Well, I don't
know why, because real live water balloons are the

easiest things in the world to balance. Watch this! *(She throws the balloon high into the air, holds her arms out to catch it, misses, and gets plastered. On cold days, or days when she just doesn't feel like getting wet, she lets the balloons hit the floor.)*

Gosh! What happened? I thought real live water balloons were the easiest things in the world to balance! Hmm. Maybe I need some more practice. *(MERRY MELODY picks up a pan that holds the remaining balloons. One is filled with water; the others, air. She displays the pan to the audience, letting them think all the balloons are filled with water. She sets the pan down and pulls the one water balloon from it, and tries her high-flight balancing act again. She misses, of course, but this time the balloon lands on the ground close to the children, who squeal and scramble.)* Darn again! This practice is getting kind of messy, isn't it? I think that instead of practicing, I'll do the real thing! I'll balance ALL of these water balloons at one time! How about that? *(Ignoring a unified negative reply)* You like it, huh? Well, all right! *(She picks up the pool cue and casually checks to see if it's straight. One end is set on the ground while she tries to balance it. Failing, she then attaches the pan of balloons to the top of the cue in such a manner as to make the audience think she's balancing the pan, not attaching it. She talks to divert attention away from her actions.)*

I'm going to balance all of these water balloons on this pan. And then I'm going to balance the pan on the end of this pool cue. And then . . . AND THEN! I'm going to walk right over there, right where everybody's sitting, and balance the pool cue on my chin and do a square dance! In circles! *(MERRY MELODY lifts the pool cue slowly and cautiously while people scramble for safety, laugh, and groan, not necessarily in that order.)* What are you worried about? I won't drop these real live water balloons on you. Yick! It would be terrible if I did, because each balloon is filled with water mixed with mud, bugs, slime, moss, and slippery little fish that like to bite. You wouldn't want me to drop all of that on you, would you? *(She walks into the middle of the audience, close to the back rows where the adults are sitting, and starts to lift the cue.)* Here we go. Right on my old chinny-chin-chin!

(The pan is high in the air when she begins to lose control. Back and forth it sways, despite her most earnest efforts. She runs everywhere with the cue, making sure no one feels safe. Chaos reigns. Finally, though, MERRY regains control. She sighs and wipes her brow — and again loses balance! This time, the inevitable happens: The balloons fall onto the heads of the children! What with all their screaming and jumping, it takes them a moment to realize the balloons are filled with air, not water.)

Ha! I sure fooled you guys, didn't I? Those weren't real live water balloons, they were my unbalancing balloons! And they worked, too, because you look pretty wobbly to me!

Tug of War

Props: A large, loose-fitting jacket or overcoat and a length of rope at least twenty feet long.

Comments: Noticing that the children are getting a bit antsy, Smiling Sam decides to let them expend some energy. He steps out of view for a moment and returns wearing his large, baggy coat, and with a coil of rope in each hand. What the children don't see is that the coils are connected: A length of rope travels through the arms and shoulders of the coat! What's that smiling Smiling Sam got in mind?

●●●●●

Smiling Sam: OK! Time for a contest! Everybody get in a line! *(SMILING SAM directs the formation of a single long line.)* Good. Now, I've got two pieces of rope. We're going to see if you're strong enough to pull the rope out of my hands. Do you — not yet, get back in line! Do you guys think you can do that? You do, huh? Well, doggone, you're probably right. *(Excitedly)* Wait a minute! I've got a brain wave lapping at my head — or heading at my lap, I'm not sure. We'll see who can pull the rope out first, the people with skinny feet, or . . . the people with FAT FEET! *(Not wasting time explaining, he looks down at the first child and judges his pulling power.)* Skinny-boned feet! Get on my left, over there, and grab this rope. Easy there! Don't start pulling until I give the word! *(One by one he determines sides, trying to keep them at fairly equal strengths.)* You've got the fattest feet I've seen in three and a half days, not to mention Sunday of last week! Wow! On my right!

Child: *(Girl)* But I want to be with my friend over there! And my feet aren't fat!

Smiling Sam: They'll be fat if I step on them. On my right, let's go! *(She obeys reluctantly. SMILING SAM turns to the very last child, another girl.)* Boy oh boy — er, I mean, girl oh girl! You've got one fat foot and one

27

skinny foot! Where do I put you? *(Thoughtfully)* Let's see . . . can you say crumplegunch?

Little Girl: Crumplegunch!

Smiling Sam: Too bad. I feel sorry for you. On my left! *(With the teams decided, SMILING SAM grabs the rope and plants his feet. Though the children, a little over-anxious, have begun to pull, SMILING SAM tries to make it sound official.)* Everybody ready? Get set! Don't pull! Whoa! *(Both teams begin pulling with all their strength, hoping to be the first to pull a rope from his hands. While they're actually tugging against each other, SMILING SAM does his best to make them think otherwise. He grunts and groans and gasps.)*

You guys are stronger than my grandma! I think my fingers are going to pop off! Uh oh! The people with the fat feet are winning, I think! *(SMILING SAM helps the fat feets out by pulling against the skinnies. After a moment, he pulls the other direction.)* I think I thought wrong! The guys with the skinny feet are winning! Everybody pull! C'mon! Hard! Harder! That's better. Now I can take a rest! *(With those words, SMILING*

SAM slips out of his baggy coat, leaving it suspended on the rope the children are tugging away at. They've been tricked! Now SMILING SAM faces a real challenge: Trying to think of a skit that will quiet everyone down!)

Talking Clownese

I know a lot about talking! In fact, some people think I should call myself Talking Tom instead of Smiling Sam, but that's another matter. I want to talk about talking.

For the most part, talk *naturally*. Well, sure, you've got to sound like you're having fun, and a little bit theatrical, but keep your voice natural. Don't make it high and squeaky or strange and strained. You're a clown, don't forget, not a weirdo. You want to sound pleasant and friendly and chummy and not risk turning anyone off. Besides the audience, *you'll* feel more comfortable if you talk naturally, and that's important if you're to enjoy what you're doing.

What Merry Melody said about actions and gestures applies to talking, too. *Ennchuniant crlay.* What do you mean you didn't hear me? I said E N U N C I A T E   C L E A R L Y! Speak slowly and loudly, and face the audience so that people in the back row can at least read your lips. Sometimes you'll be in situations where not everyone will be able to hear you no matter how loud you yell; too much competing noise or too much distance. What to do?

31

Don't worry about it. Just do your best and hope your actions alone are enough to entertain the ear strainers in the back of the crowd.

Remember: Speak clearly, loudly, slowly (or at least not too fast!), and face the audience!

Photo Fun

Props: Everything but the kitchen sink! Start with a squirt gun, candle, flashbulb, horn, spring-loaded snake, rubber chicken, firecrackers, whistle, flash paper, balloon, bubble-blowing pipe, poster of a monkey, rubber mask, party ratchet noisemaker, and anything else you can grab. Make a large box, custom designed to hold all the gimmicks for quick, simple operation. Put the black cloth on the back of the box and a tripod beneath, and you've got yourself a clown camera!

Comments: When Merry Melody hauls out her clown camera, look out! It's lights, camera, and all kinds of action!

• • • • •

Merry Melody: *(Sadly)* You know, we're having a lot of fun here today, but sooner or later it's got to end. Your moms and dads are going to take you home, and — I'll be here all alone! Oh, poor me! If only I had something to remember you by . . . *(MERRY MELODY's eyes light* *up. She smiles wide and slaps her knees.)*

Brain Train Express! Got an idea! I'll take a picture of you! How about that? That way I'll always be able to remember you. We'll have some photo fun! *(MERRY MELODY reaches into her large box of props and carefully pulls out her clown camera, not wanting any of the dozens of specially rigged and positioned gimmicks to fall out of place. She attaches it to the tripod, which is about five feet high, high enough to easily peer into and operate gimmicks, but out of reach of most children.)* That's my own clown camera! Made right here in Clowntown. *(Pause)* I guess we're all set and ready to snap. All we need are some models . . . *(MERRY MELODY inspects the audience closely, looking for people she thinks will make good models. A good model is someone who is willing to play along and be the victim of a gag or two. Ha! She spots a perfect group! A mom and dad and their two little kids!)*

Hold on! I see a family whose lucky day has arrived. Talk about photohygenic! No, let's not talk about it. You folks right there! That's right, don't be embarrassed about being my models and having your image preserved by a clown camera for eternity! Come on up and sit on this bench where everyone can watch. *(MERRY MELODY sits them on a bench in front of the clown camera. Naturally, before going to the camera, she has a little fun getting them to strike the right pose.)* Now, Mother! What's all this giggling for? Don't you know this is a very serious occasion? This is a family portrait! Here, stick your finger in your ear. Maybe that'll help. *(MERRY MELODY scurries back to the camera, lifts the black cloth that covers the opening in the rear, and sticks her head inside. She then issues instructions, which are muffled by the camera box — and her own enunciation.)*

Rrrromber gllammicksnock! Rahoomble, rahoomble! Rrrromber gllammicksnock! *(She waits, tapping her fingers impatiently on the top of the camera. Finally, she pulls her head out and confronts her models.)*

Well? Didn't you hear me? You didn't? Weren't you paying attention? I said Rrrromber gllammicksnock! Rahoomble, rahoomble! Rrrromber gllammicksnock! *(Pretends the models understand.)* Good, that's better. Only next time do it faster! *(Back in the camera)* Boy, it's dark in here! I can't tell my f-stop from my e-go, and I know at least one of them is pretty darn big! *(She pulls out a candle, lights it, and sticks it in a hole on top of the camera. At the same time, inside the box, she lights a string of three or four firecrackers.)* That candle gives us, oh, about an f-ninety. Or maybe — *(BANG! BANG! BANG! MERRY MELODY jumps. When she's sure the explosions are finished, she sticks her head back inside and shouts "FIRE! FIRE!" She also sticks a squirt gun through a hole and shoots her models.)* Don't worry. I think that put the fire out. Hey, you guys moved! *(MERRY MELODY attends to the models, getting them back into position.)*

You're all wet! Been out in the rain, huh? *(Thoughtfully)* Say, pops, why don't you take that mask off? I've got a better idea. Here, stick this pipe in your mouth and look distinguished. Don't just sit there, blow bubbles! *(MERRY rushes to the camera and cranks the party ratchet a few times. She puts her head in the camera and reaches for the "lens," which is a can nailed to the camera, containing a spring loaded snake! The "snake in a can" prop is commonly sold by novelty mail-order houses.)* Everything looks fuzzy to me. Some people think that's because my brain is fuzzy, but I think it's because the lens needs adjustment. *(MERRY MELODY takes the l-o-n-g-e-s-t time adjusting the lens! The models see her twisting the lid on the can and know something is going to happen. Finally — BOING! The snake flies out and the models fly up. MERRY looks out, slightly annoyed, and squirts the water gun a few more times. She ducks back inside and blows up a balloon which she lets go. As it zips through the air, she blows a whistle. Dazed, she steps out.)* What's going on? This place is going crazy! I never thought it would cause so much trouble just to take a simple picture, did you? *(She looks inside the camera, frowns, and pulls out a rubber chicken. She gives it a double take and throws it over her shoulder.)*

We'd better get this picture taken so you can go home and I can get some peace and quiet! Are my models ready? Good. Say cheese, please! *(She pulls out some flash paper and touches it to the candle — POOF! Casually, she puts her other hand inside the camera and grabs a horn.)* Now we wait for the film to develop. We had some good models, didn't we? I've never heard anyone say cheese so perfectly. I'll bet you're professionals, aren't you? *(MERRY MELODY toots the horn a few times and sticks her head back in the camera.)* Looks like the film is ready! Holy Moly! What a great photograph! I think I'm going to win an Emmy for this one! *(She steps out of the camera holding a rolled-up poster, which she slowly and carefully unravels. The poster is a picture of a group of monkeys dressed in human clothes.)* How about that for a family portrait?! There's Mom, there's Dad — or wait, maybe that's Dad and that's Junior — no, wait, maybe — aw, I can't tell. They all look pretty silly, though, don't they?

Juggle and Hide

Props: Bean bags, rubber balls, pool balls and, of course, rubber chickens.

Comments: Anyone and their grandmother can juggle at least two objects: Throw one in the air to a point slightly above your head. When it starts to fall, throw the next. *Simple!* Juggling three objects is a bit more tricky, but can be learned by most enthusiastic students, especially when aided by someone who knows how, or by a good instruction book. If you don't have the interest in learning to juggle three objects, don't worry. You can adapt all the gags in this routine to work wonderfully with two-object juggling!

•••••

(SMILING SAM, with a sprightly hop and skip, moves to the front of the audience and takes a ball from his pocket. The ball is a wooden croquet ball, painted red. He tosses it from hand to hand and behind his back and — BANG! He drops it on the floor. No mistake about it, that's a hard ball.)

Smiling Sam: Oops! Good thing I wasn't standing beneath the ball. I'd be Sore Sam if I were! Maybe I'd have better luck with two . . . *(He pulls another croquet ball from his pocket which is identical to the first. He juggles these about in a simple pattern — and drops both of them. BANG! BANG!)* Have you ever heard such loud, noisy balls? They hurt my ears! Maybe they'll be quieter if I juggle *three* balls! Why not? *(He pulls a third red ball from his pocket. It's the same size as the croquet balls, but it's made of rubber. SMILING SAM juggles the three balls flawlessly through the air, not dropping any of them.)* Hey, pretty good! Juggling three wooden balls is easier than juggling two or one! *(Showing off a little, he throws the rubber ball high and smacks the croquet balls together, wincing as they connect. He repeats this procedure a few more times, always making sure he* *throws the rubber ball high. The audience can't tell one ball from another, especially when they're being juggled, and assumes all three are hard, wooden croquet balls.)* Now for the big trick! This takes a lot of thought, so be real quiet while I use my head. *(The crowd quiets as SMILING SAM throws the rubber ball higher than ever before. It hurtles back down and hits him right on the head — at the same instant he smacks the two croquet balls together. He grabs the rubber ball on the rebound, before it hits the ground, and staggers about.)* Ouch! That smarts, even on a dumb head like mine. I've got to learn to be more careful, or — I'll end up like these!

(Quickly moving on to the next part of the routine, SMILING SAM sets the balls aside and grabs three rubber chickens. He's added a short length of broomstick [eighteen inches, straight down the beak!] to their anatomy so they can be juggled like clubs. No one understands why rubber chickens are funny, especially when juggled, but the fact remains that they are. SMILING SAM juggles away.) Rubber chickens! They're flying better now than they did when they were alive! Although they did fly pretty well when I tried plucking their feathers out! *(SMILING SAM drops a chicken and, frustrated, knocks himself in the head a few times with the ones he's holding. He then picks the chicken up and resumes juggling.)* What's everybody squawking at me for, anyway? This is my dinner! I'm just trying to tenderize the meat, that's all. *(A look of horror)* Uh oh! I just thought of something! What if these chickens decide to lay eggs while I'm juggling them? *(Laughing)* At least the eggs will come out scrambled! Oh, all right, I'm sorry, I'm sorry. *(To cover for his atrocious humor, he tosses the chickens over his back, continues juggling nothing, finally realizes what he's doing, and sheepishly moves on to the next part. SMILING SAM picks up three rubber balls and juggles them.)*

I know what you're thinking. I know *exactly* what you're thinking. You're thinking, sure, this clown can juggle three balls, but — *but!* Can he do three in one hand? Well, watch this! Three in one hand! Are you ready? Here we go! *(SMILING SAM stops juggling and puts all three balls in one hand — where he holds them. He points to the balls, then himself, with great pride. Unfortunately, he draws more groans than applause.)* Boy, sometimes you can't please anyone. I said I was going to do three in one hand, and I did. Oh, all right, what else have we got? How about if I juggle backwards? Would that make you happy? *(SMILING SAM's idea of juggling backwards is to turn his back to the audience and juggle. He looks over his shoulder and grins.)*

OK, no more tricks. Time for some real fancy juggling. I'm going to juggle not three, not four, not even five balls. For that matter, I'm not going to juggle six balls or seven balls, either. What I'm going to do is juggle *eight* balls, all at the same time! *(SMILING SAM walks over to his prop box and reaches down for the balls. He grabs them, but keeps them out of view of the audience.)* You don't think I can do it, do you? What can I say? Some people recognize true talent, and some don't. Believe it or not . . . eight balls at one time! *(SMILING SAM immediately begins juggling three black number eight pool balls. More groans from the audience. SMILING SAM chuckles.)* Don't everyone applaud at once — it'll ruin my concentration. *(People clap, and he immediately drops the balls. Undaunted, he reaches into the prop box and, with apparent great effort, takes out an armful of small rubber balls. He seems to have great difficulty holding the balls in his arms.)*

Juggling eight balls was just a warm-up exercise. Now I'm going to juggle *nine* balls — and I don't know how I'm going to do that, because I'm having problems just holding them. You kids better stand back in case I drop a half dozen or so. We can't take any chances on such a dangerous, challenging trick! Nine balls, and away we go! *(Well, there are nine balls, but they are grouped in tight clusters of three by means of a wire inserted through their centers. Hardly a legitimate nine-*

ball juggle. SMILING SAM shrugs and tosses them aside.) I'm sorry, but I've done my best. I've juggled three balls, eight balls, and nine balls. I've even plucked up the courage to juggle rubber chickens, but still you're not satisfied. Maybe I'm not good enough. Maybe — maybe I need some help! You! *(SMILING SAM quickly points to a child, runs over, grabs him, and drags him to the front of the audience.)*

You're going to help me juggle. Now, we've got to think of something really special, really exciting, really . . . *dangerous.* Something this audience will appreciate. Any ideas? No? Too bad. That means I have to think of something — and you know how good my ideas are. *(SMILING SAM sallies over to his prop box and sees something that catches his fancy. He pulls out a few eggs.)* We're in luck! I don't have to think! Our problems are over easy. The chickens laid eggs for us to juggle! What? You don't want to juggle eggs? Oh, but it'll be easy. I've got to do all the hard work. I throw them and you catch them. Still don't like the idea? OK, OK, we'll use bean bags instead. *(SMILING SAM has the child stand straight with his arms extended and eyes shut. He then stands behind him and juggles the bean bags, occasionally placing one on the boy's head and picking it up with the other hand. It's a simple trick, but the crowd thinks it's challenging and applauds.)* Keep those eyes shut! Concentrate! Don't drop any! *(Pause)* See, I knew with you up here helping me we'd come up with a trick they'd like!

MERRY
MELODY'S
MUSINGS

Practice Prefect Sakes
Prafect Perctice Smakes
Practice Makes Perfect

Practice may not make you absolutely perfect, but it'll make you pretty darn close. At the very least, practice gets rid of a lot of jitters and bugs and glitches before you perform.

If you're doing your first show, pick out three or four skits from this book. Which ones? The ones that appeal to you most! If you think they're funnier than the others (I think mine are funnier than Smiling Sam's, but that's just *my* opinion), then they'll be the ones you'll feel most confident performing.

After you've decided which skits, collect all the needed props (more on collecting later) and begin practicing. Read aloud from the book a few times, follow the instructions, and *pretend* an audience is watching you. Do this until you've memorized the entire skit. Keep practicing until you can perform the skit without pause. Drag a friend in off the street and get him to watch and make a few comments. Keep practicing, practicing, practicing, practicing. . . .

Until you can't put it off any longer. Get out and perform a real show! Take it from me, the experience of one real show is worth the experience of ten practice shows in your basement.

Digital Portrait Drawing

Props: A pencil and a pad of paper.

Comments: All right, maybe Merry Melody's portrait photography wasn't so hot. But she can't do any worse *drawing* portraits, can she?

Merry Melody finds this is a nice routine for prolonged one-on-one entertainment. She can wander from person to person, or family to family, spend some time with them, get to know them (and more important, let them know her), and have a lot of fun in the process. You can do the same, even if you don't know how to draw portraits (neither does Merry Melody!).

●●●●●

(MERRY MELODY walks back and forth in front of the audience with her arms stretched out, "framing" different people's faces. Sometimes she smiles, sometimes she grimaces.)

Merry Melody: Looks pretty good, pretty good. Maybe a little — oh! Hey, I bet you don't even know what I'm doing, do you? I'm framing each and every one of you. You haven't experienced life until you've been framed by Merry Melody, let me tell you. What?! No, this isn't a frame-up for something bad, it's a frame-up for something good. I figured that since my clown camera wasn't working so nifty, I'd — are you ready? — draw portraits of each and every one of you! How about that! *(While the audience contemplates the possible consequences, MERRY pulls out a huge pencil and a pad of scratch paper. At this point, she begins moving from group to group, entertaining them on a personal basis. Naturally, if this were a large, formal show with a stage and a captive audience, MERRY MELODY would either leave this routine behind or adapt it as she felt was necessary.)*

Say, you folks look like you're ready to be framed. You weren't quite photogenic enough to sit for the clown camera, but I think you're portraitgenic enough for the quickdraw. *(MERRY MELODY snaps her pencil out and holds it like a six-gun, quickly firing off a couple of rounds. She blows the smoke from the end and laughs.)* "Quickdraw," get it? No? Oh, all right, no more punning around. It's time we got down to the business at hand. Portrait drawing! *(MERRY spots a likely subject, a little girl, and adjusts her head and body for the best pose. Nothing silly, like fingers in the ear, going on here. MERRY MELODY takes her artistic skills very seriously.)* You'll make a good subject if you can just hold still. I'm a good artist, I'll have you know. I was trained as a cubist and neo-dadist, but in recent years I've developed my own style — avant-clownist! You'll like what you see, believe me! *(MERRY MELODY stands back and begins drawing. She holds her thumb out and squints, searching for the proper perspective. Her thumb is out in front of her almost constantly. In fact, MERRY spends more time swinging her thumb around than she does drawing — and manages to look silly in the process.)* All right! Enough of that. You're going to have to quit laughing if you want me to get a good rendition. When you laugh you move, and when you move and I draw, everything comes out squiggly and blurry. *(MERRY MELODY continues to draw and*

make use of her thumb. She does everything to get a better perspective. She climbs on tables, chairs, beneath tables and chairs, leans on people's backs, bends down and looks through her legs — but always using her thumb. During these antics, the little girl tries not to smile and laugh. She doesn't succeed, but she tries.)

I know clowns aren't supposed to say this, but don't laugh! We're almost finished and I wouldn't want anything to go wrong. Avant-clownist art is very delicate. I'm not trying to butter up my skills, but there's simply no margarine for error. Not one slice! *(MERRY MELODY carefully moves her thumb around, looking for what only an avant-clownist can look for. She brings her thumb closer to her face — boink! She accidentally sticks it in her eye. Worse than that, she can't get it out!)* Yeeooww! Thumbthing is in my eye. It's stuck! Somebody help me get it out. You! Pull! Harder! *(Unboink!)* Whew! Thanks, fella. I think that about does it for this portrait. All I've got left to do is put my signature on it. Let's see . . . Merry Melody. *(Signs and spells.)* Q-p-a-s-f-x-nineteen-r-w-double-me-l-a-b-c-period. Merry Melody! *(MERRY MELODY tucks her pencil away and folds the portrait in half so that no one can see. Before giving it to the little girl, she makes sure she understands*

her instructions.) This is just for you! Don't show it to anyone! And if you keep it for two hundred years, it'll be worth millions! A classic avant-clownist portrait! *(As if passing a great secret, she hands the portrait to the little girl. The little girl quickly opens it — and groans!)* Remember what I said! Don't show it to anyone! *(MERRY MELODY holds her thumb out and searches for new subjects. If you want to know what the portrait looked like, look below, but make sure your thumb is out so you can get a proper perspective on it.)*

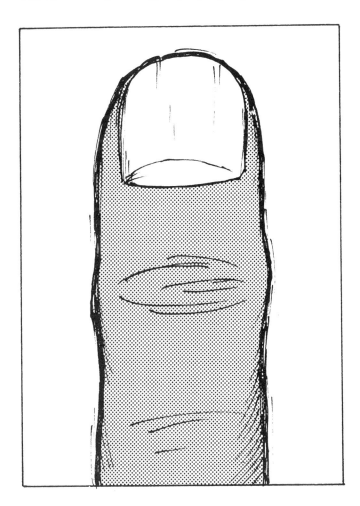

A Man Called Sam

Props: Salt and pepper shakers, gardening fork, teacup, bicycle tire, brush, squirt bottle, mirror, bone, old pair of pants, giant sunglasses, cardboard cutout of the number seven, curtain, cardboard box, plastic flower with a large, fake root, rubber duck, wind-up snapping teeth, old shoe, paper airplane, books, handful of paper punches, and finally, a light bulb. Also, a cue card for the assistant.

Whenever possible, try to use "clown-style" props instead of the real thing. For instance, instead of a small salt shaker, use a large pitcher with a bright blue "S" painted on the side. Check through novelty house supply catalogs and magic stores for big, fun props, too.

Comments: Smiling Sam always saves this stupendous routine for a captive audience that will appreciate its almost theatrical nature. He also makes sure he has a chance to talk to his helper (a volunteer, or draftee, from the audience) before the routine, and work out all the details and practice lines. Smiling Sam also lines up the props on the floor so that he and his assistant can grab them quickly and without confusion. Without further ado, Smiling Sam assumes the role of a stuffy old colonel and begins.

● ● ● ● ●

Smiling Sam: *(Startled by audience)* Hark and forsooth! You have taken me by surprise, oh my faithful audience. I truly did not expect anyone to be watching me whilst ensconced in deep ruminations. I — but I am discourteous. I should perhaps first introduce myself and my companion. I am known far and wide as —

A Friend Called Fred: Short and narrow.

Smiling Sam: — A Man Called Sam! Not simply Sam, or Sam the Man, but . . . A Man Called Sam! My companion is none other than A Friend Called Fred! Not merely Fred, or Friendly Fred, but . . . A Friend Called Fred! *(FRED moves forward and takes a deep bow.)*

A Friend Called Fred: Thank you, A Man Called Sam!

Smiling Sam: You're so welcome, A Friend Called Fred! *(SMILING SAM, annoyed with FRED getting attention from the audience, quickly yanks him back.)* Er, as I was saying. Your presence startled me as I was reliving in my mind an old but memorable adventure I had with A Friend Called Fred. It happened at the time that our nation, Clowntown, was faced with combating the peril of . . . The Enemy Called Them! Allow me to recount our adventure . . . *(FRED goes into a panic, shaking his head and waving his arms.)*

A Friend Called Fred: Not that story! Not again! My heart won't take it! Please, no! No!

Smiling Sam: Cease your immature behavior! We must share the adventure with our audience. The story must not be forgotten.

A Friend Called Fred: But if everybody remembers, why are we doomed to repeat it so often?

Smiling Sam: *(Ignoring the question)* It was early in the conflict against The Enemy Called Them. We stood valiantly against their assaults. *(On the last word, FRED pulls out a salt shaker and shakes salt on the head of SMILING SAM. Throughout the routine, the assistant will do his best to match actions with SMILING SAM's words for effective verbal/visual puns. SMILING SAM gives the assistant timing cues by pointing, winking, and employing other gestures.)*

We were peppered *(Pepper shaker is shaken)* with abuses day and night. There was no question in my mind but that we were forked in. *(Garden fork is held aloft.)* Now, I was a brave man. I was known then, as now, as A Man Called Sam! I had at my side, A Friend Called Fred. *(FRED points to himself.)* But in front of me, behind me, all around and everywhere, was The Enemy Called Them! It was not my cup of tea. *(Teacup, with water, is tasted and then dumped by FRED.)* And if that weren't enough, I was but scantily attired. *(Bicycle tire is placed over his head.)* My problem was compounded when it soon began to rain. *(Water is squirted from a bottle. SMILING SAM pauses to wipe away the*

50

water which FRED, a mere assistant, so gleefully squirted over him, and to remove the bicycle tire.)

As I was saying — before the ambience was ruined — things looked most dreadful. But then, deep in my higher consciousness, without warning, there sounded a warning. *(Horn is blown.)* I realized that I had to do something or all would be forever lost for all of Clowntown. I quickly brushed up *(Gets scrubbed with old brush)* on my battle skills and gave myself, the one and only, A Man Called Sam, a critical self-inspection. *(A mirror is held high.)* At last, I began to see. *(Giant sunglasses are placed on his face, then removed.)* The truth was, we didn't have a chance. We, A Man Called Sam and A Friend Called Fred, were goners. My number was up. *(Cutout of number seven is held high.)* It didn't matter how much we wanted to defeat The Enemy Called Them, we were boxed in. *(Cardboard box is placed over his head.)* I was facing the final curtain. *(A shower curtain is draped over his shoulder.)* Suddenly, they charged! They had seemingly outwitted us, and, with professional respect, I had to take my hat off to them. *(Hat is placed on his head which he removes.)* But in doing so, I saw something that made me feel light with hope. *(Light bulb is held over his head.)* I perceived that we might indeed have a route of egress. Yes, an escape route! *(SMILING SAM looks at his assistant expectantly, but he just stands there. He speaks*

again loudly. But the assistant, having been briefed prior to the routine, waits for his cue before moving.)

I perceived that we might indeed have discovered an escape . . . ROUTE! *(Assistant jumps to life and pulls out an old, withered bone.)* Listen here, A Friend Called Fred! I don't mean to chew an old bone, but you never get this part right! I want the escape route! Route! Route! *(SMILING SAM bends down and picks up a plastic flower with a large fake root attached to the bottom. It's pretty silly looking [just try to make a fake root!], and SMILING SAM, along with the audience, realizes it.)*

All right, never mind the escape route! Remember, The Enemy Called Them was soon to prove victorious! As they charged our perimeter, I could hear their tired, breathless pants. *(Pair of pants is thrown into his arms.)* Boldly, we made our escape, moving with the speed of a flock of geese. *(Rubber duck is held high, horn is blown, duck gets thrown.)* The Enemy Called Them charged after us, snapping at our heels. *(Assistant holds pair of tennis shoes, while SMILING SAM holds the snapping teeth.)* We would have been captured, had I not been, as I am now, A Man Called Sam. I thoughtfully arranged to have waiting for us an airplane! *(Paper airplane is thrown.)* We flew away, but entered a terrible snowstorm. *(Paper punches are thrown high.)* We had to crash land near one of my favorite hotels. Fortunately, it wasn't booked up solid. *(Stack of books is held high.)* I said, WASN'T booked up solid. *(Books are dropped on SMILING SAM's toes.)* OUCH! *(Pause — assistant sneaks away.)* Thus ends the recounting of our adventure. Always, when one lives the type of life that I, A Man Called Sam, lives, there are dangers. But with a friend like A Friend Called Fred, I know I will never be alone. *(SMILING SAM turns to pat FRED on the back, sees him sneaking offstage, and gives chase.)* Where are you going? I want to tell the story about the knife throwers of New Guinea! Come back!

SMILING SAM'S SECRETS

Relax and Be Yourself

Merry Melody has said it twice, I've said it once, and I'll say it again: When performing as a clown, relax and be yourself! I'm only telling you this so often because it's so darn important. If you're all nervous and try to cover up by exhibiting a phony, unnatural character, even my fantastic, incredibly funny, and hilarious skits won't work for you, and I'd hate to see that! I want people all over the world to laugh at my skits, and the only way that'll happen is if you do the job right!

I'm not saying that when you give your first show you should be so mellow you melt, but you should be optimistic and hope for a good time. I'll give you some more hints later on (and Merry Melody will probably have her two cents worth too!) as to what to expect in performance situations and how to deal with it, but that's not important right now. What's important is that you start out on the right foot and don't trip! So follow me and YIKES! Ooops! Whoooaaa! Ouch! I'll tell you what, you go on ahead and I'll catch up with you.

Remember: Relax, be natural, and have a good time.

Baaaaaaalloooooons!

Props: A handful of long, skinny balloons and a hand pump (or a good set of lips and lungs).

Comments: The way Merry Melody figures, no clown act is complete without some fun with balloons. Sad (but true), Merry Melody, like many other clowns, doesn't know how to make animals and whatnot out of the long balloons. Happily, that doesn't stop her from having a good time.

• • • • •

(MERRY MELODY waves a handful of empty balloons through the air. In her other hand is the small balloon pump. It doesn't take the kids long to catch on that they're going to be getting some goodies to play with.)

Merry Melody: Baaaaalloooooons! Baaaaalloooooons! Everybody line up for a free baaaaalloooooon! Moms and dads and kids and grandmas! We got baaaaalloooooons for everybody here! Who's first? Yikes! Everybody's first, huh? We'll start with the last person then. *(MERRY MELODY singles out a young boy and blows up a balloon for him. It's long and skinny and shiny — and untied. When she hands it to him she makes sure she releases it before he actually grabs it. ZIP! It flies through the air.)* What's the big idea? Hold on to the darn thing! *(She pumps up another and hands it to him, again untied. When it flies away she shakes her head and pumps up a third. She doesn't tie it, but does make sure the boy clamps his fingers around the end. He holds on for dear life, afraid it'll blow away like the others.)* That'll keep you busy, won't it? When you get it figured out, come back and tell me, because I'd sure like to know! *(MERRY MELODY next uses a balloon that has been specially prepared. Prior to the show she took a needle and poked a tiny hole in the closed end. She pumps it up and quickly ties it, then puts it into one of many outstretched hands.)*

Hold this balloon and hold your breath. *(The balloon rapidly deflates in front of the child's eyes. MERRY takes another prepared balloon and repeats the process. Again the balloon deflates. She takes a third prepared balloon and pumps it up, but instead of handing it to anyone, she lets it fly up to the ceiling. With the tiny hole in it, it slowly bounces and dances for about ten seconds before deflating and falling to the ground. She finally pumps up a good balloon and gives it to the frustrated child.)* This time make sure you hold your breath, or the same thing will happen! *(MERRY MELODY spots a young toddler who isn't quite sure what to make of all this clown business.)* Hey! A halfakid! You know what I make special for halfakids? Halfaballoons! *(MERRY MELODY pumps a balloon half full, ties it, and hands it to the toddler. The toddler isn't quite*

sure what to make of the balloon, either, except that it's nice to suck on the long, uninflated half. MERRY pumps another full balloon and hands it out. It happens to fall into two different hands at once, a not uncommon occurrence at clown soirees. A minor disagreement ensues concerning ownership.)

Whoa! Hold everything! Balloons are for fun. Now I've got a whole bunch of balloons, so there's no need to fight; you'll each get one. *(Pause)* BRAIN PLANE! An idea just landed in my head. Since both of you want the same balloon, you'll both get the same one! Here, you hold one end and you hold one end. *(Making sure there's no danger, MERRY quickly whips out a sharp pair of scissors from a safe, secure pocket, and snips the balloon in half. BANG! MERRY MELODY is all action where King Solomon was all talk. And to prevent tears or revenge [of the kick-in-the-shin variety], she promptly hands out a balloon to each of the kids.)* See? Unless you guys get a bang out of fighting, it's not much fun, is it? *(MERRY hands out another dozen or so balloons before getting back to the gags. She starts talking to one little girl while absently pumping a balloon. The balloon gets bigger and bigger. Everyone seems to notice that it's getting too big — everyone but MERRY MELODY, who is busy jabbering.)*

And as I was telling my friend, Smiling Sam the clown, all the hot air in the world won't — *(BANG! Children leap and scream and cover their ears. MERRY is completely surprised and jumps about much as you'd expect a very scared clown to jump about.)* YIKES! What happened? Am I all right? Why didn't they tell me they were starting World War Three? *(Pause)* Say, what happened to my balloon? *(MERRY MELODY pumps up another balloon, slowly but surely making it as big as the previous one.)* So I made a mistake with the last balloon? Big deal. I won't make a mistake with this balloon, no sir. I'm going to be very careful. Gosh, if a second balloon were to — *(BANG! Again she's scared half out of her make-up! After calming down, she turns to the girl she was making the balloon for.)* You must be bad luck! This time, I'm really playing it safe! *(MERRY pumps a little more than an inch of the balloon, ties it and hands it to her.)* There you go. There's no way this balloon is going to explode! Ha! What? You want a bigger balloon? Oh, all right, I guess that's fair. How about a world-famous Merry Melody sculpture? *(MERRY MELODY is one of those rare artists who can apply avant-clownism to all mediums. This time, she ties a long balloon into a knot.)* Own this balloon with pride. It's a self-portrait. *(She promptly ties a dozen more balloons into identical knots, describing them as elephants, rocks, flowers, butterflies, metaphysical conceptualizations, the big bang theory, dogs, kittens, etc. Like she says, when it comes to avant-clownism, it's all in how you look at it.)*

The Clown Copper

Props: An optional, but very entertaining prop is a cardboard box police car that can be worn around the waist! Find a box approximately 24 inches by 36 inches. Cut a hole in middle of the length that is big enough for your waist, and attach some suspenders or bungee cords to the box so you can hang it on your shoulders. Paint it black and white. Write "Clown Copper" on the sides. You're ready to roll!

You'll also want a whistle, a flashlight, a pen and a pad of paper, and a squirt gun. If you can find a dark coat and some kind of police hat, you'll have a great costume. Top it all off with a badge and you're a clown copper!

Comments: Like "Photo Fun" and "Baaaaallooooons!" this is a good routine to use in informal performance situations. Everyone can watch, yet you are still able to work one-on-one with audience members.

●●●●●

(SMILING SAM struts out in his brand spanking new police car and uniform. He is one tough cop.)

Smiling Sam: Listen up and listen good. I'm the cop of Clowntown. I aim to do my job and to do it right. I've got a gun and I know how to use it! *(He brandishes his squirt gun menacingly — and accidentally squirts himself in the eye.)* Er, right where I aimed it. I never miss. If you're smart, you won't make me prove it. If you're not stupid, you won't make me chase you. I catch everybody I chase when I drive this hot rod. I can turn on a dime and stop on a nickel. I can — oops! *(SMILING SAM slips and crashes to the floor. He hurriedly gets up and brushes his car clean.)* Just a minor fender bender, that's all. Nothing to worry about, especially when I've got to get to work. Hey, you! How come you're not laughing? Don't you know it's a law in Clowntown that everyone has to laugh? *(At this point, the child begins giggling uncontrollably.)* Come on, I've seen that trick a thousand times. Laughing now won't help. I saw you a minute ago and you were clearly not laughing. I'm afraid I'll have to write you up for this. *(SMILING SAM scribbles something on his pad and hands it to the boy. SMILING SAM shakes his head sadly.)* I hope this serves as a valuable lesson. Don't let it happen again. *(SMILING SAM looks around the crowd for another criminal. He takes his flashlight out and aims it at different people, studying, searching for clues.)*

You! That's right, you! What the heck do you think you're doing with a face like that? Don't you know that faces like yours are considered illegal? No, I guess you wouldn't. Here's a ticket. Don't give me any more problems. *(SMILING SAM hands the poor soul a ticket and tries to back up, but he gets stuck between some people. He can't move!)* I knew I should have bought some new tires! I'm stuck! Somebody help push me! There we go. Free once again to hunt down wanton criminals! Hey, there goes one now! *(SMILING SAM blows his whistle and begins running. Round and round he goes, and where he stops nobody knows! Finally, he settles in on his victim. He chuckles.)* Thought you could get away from Smiling Sam, eh? Ha! You thought wrong, buddy. You also thought wrong when you decided to quit laughing. No one quits laughing when I'm in town. What do you mean, you know that? Wise guy, huh? I oughta lock you up in the clinker. But I feel like a nice guy today, know what I mean? So I'm only going to give you a double penalty for not laughing. *(SMILING SAM looks into the eyes of the audience members.)*

That's right, keep laughing and don't stop. You, there. Pick it up a little. Giggling doesn't count, and neither does a big smile. To stay legal, I need to hear you laughing. Big laughs. Come on, this is serious business. No fooling around. I'll be back and check on you later. Right now I've got to patrol another area. *(SMILING SAM puts his car in gear. Something's not right. It starts bucking, turning uncontrollably, going too fast, slamming on the brakes, popping up on its rear wheels, driving over tables and chairs, spinning in circles, and in general not acting at all like a car should act!)* Look out! I can't stop it! I knew I shouldn't have put kickapoo juice in the old gas tank! No telling what she'll do! Whoa! Look out! *(He finally crashes to a stop against a wall and regains control. He turns and looks at the audience, which is now laughing with genuine enthusiasm. SMILING SAM doesn't like this.)* You're not laughing at me, are you? Hold on a moment! That wasn't funny! I was scared! I was riding a wild car and you think it's funny! I hate to tell you this, but it's illegal to laugh at me when I'm scared. I'm going to have to give everybody tickets! *(He looks at his ticket pad and frowns. He counts the criminals and then counts the tickets.)* Not enough tickets for everybody. Too bad. I'll tell you what I do have enough of, though. WATER! One squirt for everyone! *(SMILING SAM squirts at random, giving everyone a couple of good sprinkles of water before hanging up the badge!)*

Start Out Simple

When I started out as a clown, I was ready to set the world on fire! LOOK OUT, I shouted, HERE COMES MERRY MELODY. I ended up getting burned.

Clowning isn't the hardest thing in the world. I mean, *anyone* can do it, as long as they have the desire and enjoy what they're doing, but it's not the easiest thing in the world, either. You've got to start out with your feet planted firmly and take one step at a time, not one big jump.

The first skit I performed was a long one with lots of silent action that depended more on a well-developed character than on funny lines and gags. I wanted to perform it because it looked so exciting! Well, it is exciting *now* (since I've learned to become a great clown!), but it was a little over my head when I started. After that first experience I began performing just one or two simple skits. Each performance afterward I added another skit. One step at a time. Before I knew it, I had a ninety-minute show! I never could have started out with a ninety-minute show (not a good one, that is!).

Remember: Start out simple and slowly, confidently, steadily work your way up!

The Haunted Ha Ha's

Props: The most important prop is a large curtain about six feet high by four feet wide that you'll have to hide yourself and your props behind. You can either hang it from the ceiling or attach a pole across the top length and have a friend hold it up, or rig together some kind of stand. You might find a large cardboard box (some water heater boxes will work) that you can cut out and make work as well as a curtain. It stands by itself!

You'll also need a cuddly teddy bear, a large white bedsheet, a black sock, a bright flashlight, and a pair of sunglasses.

Comments: The only trick to this routine is making sure your curtain or box hides your entire body. No noses or toes or bottoms should stick out!

• • • • •

(MERRY MELODY walks up to the curtain and frowns. She's afraid to go very near it and keeps her distance. There's something about this curtain that she just doesn't like.)

Merry Melody: I'm not sure, but I think this is the famous haunted curtain that everyone's been telling me about. *(Shudders with fear.)* I'm ascared! I'm ascared! *(MERRY looks at the audience and sees that no one else is frightened of the haunted curtain. This gets her goat.)* What's the matter with you guys, aren't you scared? You're not? Well, gee, maybe I shouldn't be scared either. Do you think I should go inside and see what's there? *(Of course they do! MERRY MELODY takes a big gulp and slowly and nervously approaches the curtain. She peers behind it but can't see a thing, even with her eyes squinted. She leans over further to get a better look and starts to fall. With a lot of arm waving she catches her balance and jumps away from the curtain.)* Yikes! I almost fell into the haunted curtain! It's so dark in there I can't see a thing. Maybe if I use my flashlight it won't be so haunted or dark! *(She pulls a* *flashlight out of her pocket and looks again behind the curtain. But what's this? She's got the flashlight aiming the wrong direction! The bright light is pointed directly into her eyes. Her eyes are so squinted she can't see a thing. She solves the problem by putting on a pair of sunglasses.)* That's better! In fact, I don't even need the light, it's so bright in there. *(Discards flashlight.)* I guess this isn't so scary after all. Say, what's this? *(She reaches behind the curtain and grabs something. YIKES! What is it? Her mouth falls open and her knees shake. She flips her sunglasses off. All of a sudden, the thing she's holding yanks her behind the curtain where she starts whooping and yelling.)* Whoa! It's got me! A giant monster! I'm being attacked by a giant monster! I knew this curtain was haunted! Eeeeek! Help me! *(Suddenly, MERRY tumbles out from behind the curtain, still struggling with the giant monster. She finally stands on her feet and comes to her senses, and finds that she's holding a lovable little teddy bear, not a giant monster.)*

Say! This isn't a monster, it's my teddy bear. *(She gives the teddy a hug before putting it down and going back to the curtain. She reaches inside again.)* Maybe this curtain isn't as haunted as I thought it was. Maybe . . . AAAGGGHHH! *(Something has grabbed MERRY MELODY's hands. She struggles. One minute she's pulled behind the curtain, the next she manages to step back out — but always her hands are behind the curtain.)* This is it! It's got me! This is my final curtain! I can't get away. A big, cold, slimy hand has grabbed me! It's the yickiest thing I've ever felt in my life! It's — *(She pulls away from the curtain, still struggling. She looks at her hands and sees that what she was struggling against was herself! She had grabbed her own arm! She sheepishly defends herself.)* Well, it's not that yicky, I mean . . . I haven't used my hand lotion today and. . . . *(Something behind the curtain catches her attention. She points to it and runs behind. This time she's going to catch something! After she gets behind the curtain, though, she begins to have second thoughts.)*

What am I doing? Help! Something is flying around in here and trying to bite me! *(At this point MERRY MELODY pretends to be a strange, monsterlike spirit and makes low moaning sounds. The MONSTER speaks.)*

Monster: Merrry Mellooody! I'm going to get you! I'm the vaaampire of the currrtain!

Merry Melody: Help me, somebody, anybody! There's a bat in here! A big vampire bat! It wants to suck the blood out of my foot! It's on my foot! Help!

Monster: Ohhh ha ha! I'm going to get you! Merrry Melllooody hee hee!

Merry Melody: AAAHG! The vampire bat! The vampire bat! *(MERRY comes flying out from behind the curtain with a bat flying in front of her face. Wait a minute! That's not a bat, that's a black sock she's holding in her hand, and she's flapping it up and down. When MERRY realizes this, she sighs and looks at her feet. Only one foot has on a shoe and sock. The other is bare!)* Darn! I thought sure there was something really scary back there. Maybe I'd better go check one more time. *(MERRY, despite her shaking and shivering, walks behind the curtain one more time.)*

Monster: Ooooo Ha Ha! I've got you this time, Merrry Melllooody! Ha Ha Ha! *(MERRY MELODY screams only once, and is cut short. There is a long moment of silence. Then, slowly, mysteriously, a monster, a thing, a GHOST!, creeps out from behind the curtain. MERRY MELODY is wearing a large white bedsheet. She's the MONSTER!)*

Monster: Ha Ha! I am the ghost of Merry Mellooody! I have trapped her! She's mine until the hood of the other world is removed! *(She moves out to the audience, tempting people to pull the sheet off.)*

Merry Melody: *(High, pleading voice)* Help me! Pull the sheet off and help me escape!

Monster: Yes! Only if the sheet is pulled off will she escape, but that will never happen. No one will pull the sheet off, will they? *(Hint, hint, hint . . .* No one will pull the sheet off, will they? *(Finally some brave soul gets the idea and slides off the sheet! There's MERRY MELODY.)*

Merry Melody: Oh, thank you, thank you so much! Now I'm free of that monster. I'm taking that curtain down and getting rid of it. *(MERRY takes the curtain down, but it wraps over her and she begins struggling with it. She screams for help as it drags her Offstage. That'll teach her to go peeking behind curtains!)*

Decathlon Simulcast

Props: Tennis ball and tennis racquet with no strings, golf ball and club with long elastic band, bowling ball and three pins, baseball and bat, bow and arrow, dart, boxing gloves, Floppy Flyer (or similar cloth Frisbee-like flying disk), 36-inch stick, football, and either a fake microphone or, depending on your finances and the setting, a real sound system. Again, try to keep a strong visual avant-clownist look to all of your props.

Comments: It's decathlon time in Clowntown, and Smiling Sam has entered the competition. He's also agreed to do the live broadcast of the event! It's a challenging dual role, but that's what makes clowning fun. (That, and lots of room in which to properly perform this routine.)

• • • • •

(SMILING SAM takes hold of a microphone and speaks with the voice of a gung ho, excitable sportscaster.)

Smiling Sam: Good evening, ladies and gentlemen, I'm your host on K-Clown radio and television, Smiling Sam, and tonight we have a big sports event for you, the Clowntown Decathlon! Ten sporting events brought to you live, play by play, move by move, etcetera by etcetera. If you like sports, you're tuned to the right channel. Stay tuned, we'll be right back. *(Spins around.)* And we're back! That's the kind of accurate, objective coverage you can continue to expect from K-Clown radio and television coverage of the Clowntown Decathlon. *(Seeing something in distance)* And it looks like — yes, yes! We're finally ready to begin. I've never seen anything like it before. The tension is high and the drama building — well, it's over in the fine arts complex. Hold everything! They're announcing the first contestant — why, I don't believe it. Incredible! Smiling Sam, me, I am the first contestant. *Unbelievable!* Don't worry, though, I'll continue to bring you the action objectively and passionately,

even while competing in the Decathlon. Here goes nothing! The first event is a tennis match. Smiling Sam chooses a racquet and a ball, he lines up to serve, he pulls back, he swings. . . . *(The racquet, with no strings, passes over the ball.)* And he misses! He missed the ball! *Unbelievable!* He swings again, misses! Swings, misses! I don't know what the odds are of someone missing that many serves in a row, but in Clowntown, they can't be too high. It looks like . . . yes, it's official. Smiling Sam is hanging it up in the tennis tenth of the decathlon. He figures nine more events, what the heck?

Next event, the discus! The world record is at stake here. The discus is one of Smiling Sam's specialties. He grabs hold of the discus, he concentrates, he winds up, he spins — and he throws the discus backwards! The *wrong* direction! *Unbelievable!* That gives Smiling Sam a minus twenty feet! Oh, poor guy out trying his best, and what happens, huh? How many times have we seen it? Hey, but there's still more to come. Up next, bowling, one of the great decathlon events. *(SMILING SAM sets three bowling pins up and grabs a ball. He gives himself a shake, rattle, and roll [by shaking his foot, rattling his hips, and turning a pirouette] to restore his confidence.)*

Smiling Sam looks down the lane. He stares the pins right in the eyes, daring them not to fall over. Ha! What an athlete! What a champ. Look out! He approaches the line, swings — *(The ball doesn't come out of his hands. SMILING SAM flies through the air and lands with a smack on the lane. The ball is inches from the pins.)* Tough luck! My heart goes out to the spunky little guy, but, be that as it may, he's still disqualified from this event. No matter, no matter, Smiling Sam is a great athlete who can bounce back! *(SMILING SAM grabs a volunteer and stands him up on the stage. He then picks up a dart and takes aim.)*

Ah, yes. This event is the very dignified sport of dart throwing. A couple of bull's-eyes would come in handy for this spunky competitor. Let's see how he does. Say, you know it wouldn't hurt if the target were to hold still. How can an athlete be expected to concentrate with wiggly targets? *(SMILING SAM aims, draws back for the throw and — SPLAT! He pretends to poke himself in the eye with the dart. He waves the target back to his seat. No more darts for SMILING SAM.)* Well, he misses the bull's-eye, but he does hit the clown's-eye. He'll get a few points for trying, at any rate, and he's not going to argue. He's busy getting ready for event number five, golf! Say, there's an exciting sport, I must say. My satistician tells me that if Smiling Sam can hit a hole in one, he'll still be in the running for a gold medal. Let's let the clown concentrate and watch in silence, shall we? *(SMILING SAM uses a golf club with an elastic string attached to the head. The other end of the string is attached to the ball. It's one way to make sure he always gets his ball back. He swings . . .)* So far, so good! It's a clean hit, and the ball rolls straight for the hole! It's going to drop in! It's right on the edge — *(He snaps the club back.)* Hold everything! The ball is coming back! All the way to his feet! *Unbelievable!* At this rate, it's to his advantage to take all the penalty strokes and forget about swinging! When it rains, it pours. How many times have we seen it, anyway, huh? *(SMILING SAM sets up the high-jump stick across the seats of two chairs.)*

The sixth event, the high jump! If Smiling Sam doesn't take first place in this, with those huge feet of his, then I've seen everything! And how many times have we seen that, I ask you? Here he goes, and don't be surprised if he jumps right out of this stadium! Ha! *(SMILING SAM runs for the bar, but at the last moment, instead of jumping, dives flat, and crawls under.)* What's this? He's crawling! This isn't the limbo, kid, JUMP! JUMP! Too late, he's through. Well, I don't know, maybe we shouldn't be too hard on the kid. There's a lot of pressure in the high jump. Now the next event, archery, is another matter altogether. No pressure there. The archer can take all day to make sure he aims his best. Smiling Sam at least appears to be confident, and why not? His bad luck can't continue forever. Just remember, it's not over until it's over. How many times have we seen that, I ask you? *(SMILING SAM places the arrow in his bow, pulls the drawstring, releases — releases the bow! The arrow stays in his hand!)*

Not the bow, you fool! The arrow! The — ! Ah, ha, ha, there I go, losing my objectivity! Sorry about that. OK, Smiling Sam botches the archery event. Let's see how he does in football, the great American sport. Seeing that he does have a team to play with, we can only hope he'll do better than he has on previous events. To start things off, Smiling Sam will kick the ball to the opposing team. *(SMILING SAM sets the ball on the tee and gets ready to kick. He runs up to the ball, swings his leg, and misses. What's worse, he falls on his bottom!)*

Did you see that? Can you believe it? He missed the ball! *Unbelievable!* Try as he might, this unique athlete can't seem to get it together today. What's this? He appears to be suffering from an acute case of fannyitis! We all know what that means — he'll have to pull out of the football competition. Too bad, but don't forget, baseball is next, and anything can happen. *(SMILING SAM finds an older person in the audience who can toss a baseball to him, gives him some quick instructions, and goes to bat.)*

Baseball! The national pastime, take me out to the ballpark, I don't care if I ever get back. There's no way in the world Smiling Sam can flub this up, I mean, every kid in the country knows this game. But who knows? I don't, and that's what makes sports "sporting." The pitcher winds up, he throws — *(And SMILING SAM swings and strikes, spins around, swings and strikes, keeps spinning, swings and strikes a third and final time.)* — The hitter swings, strike one! Strike two! Strike three! He's out, three strikes on one pitch! Never before have I seen such a thing! It looks like, yes! They're throwing him off the team! He can't even try out for batboy! *Unbelievable! (Pause)* We come now to the final event in the Clowntown decathlon, the one event that any big, dumb lummox can handle, boxing! Even Smiling Sam should be able to score some points in this event. But then, who knows? Anything can happen, I've never seen it before, how many times have we seen it, it's not over until it's over, and hold everything! Smiling Sam comes out swinging. If he can score a first-round K.O., OK, maybe he'll get a medal. Maybe not. What's this?! *(SMILING SAM dances around the ring, swinging at himself, dodging some punches, connecting on others.)* He's trying to knock himself out! I thought boxers were a little slow, but . . . Ouch! Stop that, that's me you're hitting! Ouch! I give up! I surrender! I — *(Smack! SMILING SAM's eyes roll back as he melts to the floor. It's a knockout. A fitting ending to an exceptionally poor showing in the annual Clowntown decathlon.)*

SMILING SAM'S SECRETS

Building and Collecting Props

"A clown is only as good as his props." I don't know if anybody famous in the clown biz ever made that remark, but it still sounds like it *should* have been made, don't you think? Take me and my skits, for instance. Sure, I have a lot of funny lines and I look pretty interesting and humorous, but I also have GREAT props. That's because I know people think a giant flyswatter is just as funny as my giant nose, or my giant smile, or my giant jokes! I put as much time and effort into building and collecting my props as I do my jokes.

Sometimes I take things that already exist and make them into funny props. Once I took a lampshade, painted it bright red and blue, and wore it for a hat. Other times I fabricate props. I made a giant book by folding a big piece of cardboard and gluing newspapers inside. Then I painted it blue and red (if you haven't guessed, those are my favorite colors — they remind me of the meals Mom used to cook!) Merry Melody and I give lots of instructions on how to build props, or where to get them. After you read through and perform a few of our skits, you'll have a good idea of what makes a good clown prop, and even how to design your own. Here are a few tips.

Allow yourself one or two tries to make the prop look exactly how you want it to look. Don't give up. Use lots of bright paint.

Generally, make things BIGGER than average. A giant handkerchief is funnier than a regular-sized handkerchief. Try to add silly, out-of-place parts to the prop. An umbrella above a bathtub, for example. Props don't have to be perfect, either. Audiences are very forgiving, as long as the props look *kind of* like what they're supposed to look like (in the same way clowns look *kind of* like regular human beans!).

You can buy a lot of props, especially if you keep your eyes open. I bought a pair of giant sunglasses in the toy section of the grocery store! If you buy from special stores or from mail-order businesses, you can get a lot of custom-designed clown props. They'll cost a little bit more money and you'll have to wait to get them, but they're usually well made and guaranteed to bring laughs.

Remember: Read our instructions and add your creativity when building props!

Magic Act

Props: A quarter, and a set of linking rings, which are inexpensive and easy to learn (if you have an extra five seconds). They can be purchased, along with many other magic props, through all magic and novelty stores and catalogs. Also available are books that will show you hundreds of easy magic tricks with rope, coins, cards, handkerchiefs, and other simple props.

Comments: Merry Melody was at first reluctant to do magic. "I'm no magician, I'm a clown." Then she realized that clowns can do anything they want and get away with it, even if it doesn't work. So, she practiced these tricks for all of thirty seconds and is already calling herself a magical clown! *Smooth.*

• • • • •

(MERRY MELODY digs into her pockets . . . deeper and deeper she digs, but with no luck. She even pulls her pockets inside out, not to mention taking her shoe off and shaking it. Nothing.)

Merry Melody: Poor Merry Melody is flat broke! I don't have a penny to my pockets, let alone my name. I know money isn't everything, but you never hear people say money isn't *something!* If I had some money, why, I'd buy a pair of shoes this big *(Holds hands ten inches apart.)* Except, I like BIG shoes. Maybe I'd get 'em this big. *(Hands two feet apart)* Or maybe . . . . *(Hands stretch all the way apart.)* Yeah! Clown-sized shoes! *(MERRY sighs and looks down at her empty pockets. She tucks them back in her pants and shuffles around, sad and depressed. But look out—)*

Cruising in the brain lane again! Got an idea! If you guys give me a hundred dollars, then I can buy some BIG shoes! How about it? No? Well, it doesn't hurt to ask. Hmmm. Say, I know how I could get some money! I can make money with magic! How about that! I sure don't have anything to lose. *(MERRY MELODY gives her audience the once-over searching for a volunteer who is fairly quiet and shy. She doesn't want some blab-bermouth who'll blurt out her magic secrets [in case she slips up]. She finally finds a helper and brings him up.)* You'll be a good helper. You've got money coming out of your ears, so it won't take very much magic to get it. *(MERRY MELODY bends his head sideways and peers into his ear. She's excited by what she sees.)* Talk about rich! You must have a million dollars and about eighty-five cents in there! Not bad. Most people with that much green stuff in their head don't have much sense, but you've got eighty-five of them! I know this is pretty taxing on you, so I'll get started with my magic before your money's gone. Clownacadabra! *(Concealing a shiny quarter in her left hand, MERRY points to her open, empty right hand. She passes her left hand over the right and smoothly and secretly transfers the quarter to the right hand. No great skills of legerdemain are required for this stunt, just a little practice with an*

*emphasis on making smooth, even motions. With the
coin now hidden in the right, she then reaches out and,
with her right hand. . . . Clownacadabra! Pulls a shiny
quarter from behind the boy's ear!)*

How about that! You've got more than carrots
growing in your ears, you've got quarters growing!
Whole bunches. I'm going to be able to buy the biggest
shoes in the world! *(MERRY pretends to drop the quarter into her pocket but keeps it hidden in her hand. She
repeats the transfer process again, proving that both
hands are empty, and pulls a quarter from the boy's
other ear. Stereo magic!)*

Thanks, partner! Don't feel too bad about good
old Merry Melody taking some money from you. As you
get older, everybody in the world's going to take your
money. Isn't that right, Dad? *(Pause)* How much money
do you think I've got in my pocket? I bet I've got close
to a million! At least eighty-five cents! *(MERRY
MELODY reaches into her pocket, digs around and —
YIKES! No money! Sadly, she slowly pulls the pocket
inside out to show everyone her bad luck.)* Easy come,
easy go! I'll just have to settle for the shoes I've got!
*(She quickly moves on to the next routine, the linking
rings. This is a fun routine because, in informal situations, she can work it individually with every child in
the audience. MERRY keeps things simple by working
with only two rings.)*

Holy matrimony! Look what Merry Melody has!
Rings! They're not wedding rings, thank goodness,
they're magic rings! *(Thoughtfully)* Besides, they're too
big to be wedding rings. And who'd marry a clown like
me, anyway? Oh well. *(She examines the rings
thoroughly, studying them for some kind of clue. She
holds them up to the audience for its inspection, but
keeps her thumb over the "secret" [a small gap in one
of the rings]. She pretends to turn the trick ring in her
hand, but merely slides one hand over the edge while
keeping the gap tightly covered. Since the ring is shiny,
smooth, and bright, the audience is easily deceived into*

thinking it is being turned.) At least, I think they're magic rings. I can't figure out what the magic is, though. Maybe I can pull a rabbit out of them! *(She puts the rings together and reaches through, groping. No luck.)* Maybe these rings will make money in my pocket! Or give me giant shoes if I step into them! Or make me a beautiful princess if I put them around my face! *(MERRY MELODY tries using the rings for each of these different schemes, but can't quite seem to make them work. She holds them together in front of her.)*

Well, at least I *felt* beautiful. Kind of. *(She sighs long and hard. Presto! She lets go of one ring and it connects [through the gap] with the other! Magic!)* What the—? They're hooked together! I blew on them and they hooked together! That must be their magic, hooking and — hey! How do I get them to unhook! I know! I'll take a deep breath! *(She does, and what do you know! They come unhooked! Not wanting to do all the hard work herself, she calls on volunteers to blow on the rings [Harder! Harder!] and to suck in air ["A big breath! Pretend you're a balloon!"]. Some volunteers aren't quite as talented, and in addition to everything else, have to cross their fingers or do whatever else MERRY happens to think of at the moment.)*

A Not So Magic Act

Props: Just your own smiling face and clever skills!

Comments: Smiling Sam didn't have time to learn normal magic as Merry Melody did. Instead, he improvised what can only be called "clown magic." If you work with the material in this routine, you'll soon find a limitless supply of similar magic tricks, any of which are perfect for filling in a transition between routines, or for getting a good laugh in the middle of a weak one.

• • • • •

(SMILING SAM rubs his hands together and does his best to look like a mysterious fellow.)

Smiling Sam: Beware! Beware one and all, for I am Smiling Sam the Sorcerer. I am a practitioner of dark and ancient magic! And tonight the moon is full and my powers are at high tide. The very earth is at my command. Prepare yourself for a full display of my powers!! *(SMILING SAM puffs his chest up and waves his arms through the air, conjuring his powers. He moves stealthily toward the nearest wall.)* I shall now move the earth in a sideways direction. Be warned! *(With his feet close to the wall, SMILING SAM leans against it and pushes. Nothing seems to be happening at first, but soon his feet begin to slide away from the wall. SMILING SAM continues pushing with all his strength until the wall is almost out of reach.)*

Hocus pocus, ergo sum! I have moved the earth! A simple task, though, one which requires little magic and lots of muscle, as well as equal amounts of suspension of belief! And now for a greater display of my magic skills! I shall spin the earth! *(SMILING SAM grabs a chair and sets it firmly on the floor. He grabs hold of the back and pretends to twist it, moving his body [not the chair] backwards until he completely circles the chair. When he finishes, he wipes his brow.)* Are you dizzy? Well, that's probably because I didn't spin the earth too fast. No matter! I call upon the spirits of magic to assist me in a most incredible display of feet! Razzamataz! *(SMILING SAM goes into a handstand.)* I have turned the earth upside-down! Don't worry! If you stay seated you won't fall off. Hold onto your tables! *(SMILING SAM starts to weaken and falter. He yells and tumbles to the ground.)*

Look out! I'm losing my upside-down magic! Here comes the earth! *(Boom!)* Whew! Enough of this earth-moving, subterranean-style magic. That's hard work! How about if we try some fun and surprising magic? *(SMILING SAM catches his breath and holds up his hands. In each hand he connects his thumb and forefinger to make a circle.)* You see before you two circles, each sealed tight. I am now going to magically connect these two circles, *without* breaking the seal! *(SMILING SAM takes a deep breath and concentrates. His arms shake as he brings his hands closer together. They touch and he strains with the magic — Presto! They're linked together. He holds the hands up for everyone to see.)*

And now, for my next trick, I'll — *(Forgetting that his hands are still connected, SMILING SAM tries to gesture with his right hand and jerks the left along with it. He tries to disconnect his hands, but has a great deal of difficulty. He can't seem to do it! Frustrated and embarrassed, he turns his back to the audience and, we are to presume, cheats. He turns around with his hands unlocked.)* Ha ha! A minor . . . technical problem with the alignment of the spirits in the. . . . How about a new trick? *(He holds both hands up, palms out, and all fingers closed except the pinky on his right hand. He moves the right hand until it touches the left. Miraculously, the pinky travels from one hand to the other. The right pinky closes and the left pops up! He repeats the process to put the pinky back on the right. SMILING SAM beams with pride.)* Pretty nifty, huh? How would you like to see that in slow motion? *(Not needing to wait for an answer, SMILING SAM brings his hands together. This time — slowly — the right pinky goes down, the right ring finger goes up, then down, the middle finger goes up — and so on, until the left pinky is standing up. He smiles and moves on. By golly, he's got magic tricks and they can't wait for applause.)*

And now, magic with an invisible string! *(He pulls the invisible string out of his pocket and threads it through an invisible needle. He pokes the needle through one eye and then the next, wincing only slightly. He ties a little knot, stretches out some more thread, and ties the end to his finger. His eyes are now attached to his finger. Everywhere the finger goes, the eyes follow. The finger moves up and down, back and forth, fast and slow, and all around, but the eyes never fail to follow. It becomes apparent that he's trying to trick his eyes with quick, jumpy half-starts and go's. As a last resort, he tries moving his finger behind his body. Boing! The string breaks and his eyes bounce around uncontrollably!)* Wowowowowowww! That smarts when the magic breaks. I think I've had enough of this physical magic. I'm ready for the ultimate! Mental magic! For that, I'll need a volunteer!

You'll do fine! Stand up here . . . good. This is mental magic, so pay attention. On this side of my head, I'm going to hold up a number, one that you choose. Go on, pick one. Any number between one and five. That's right, just pry up the right amount of thumbs and fingers . . . finished? Good. Now remember, I can't see the number, and I have no idea what it is. *(Hand is clearly on side of head where he can't see it.)* But nonetheless, I'm going to use magic to guess the number. Pay attention, and make sure I don't cheat. *(SMILING SAM concentrates with his eyes shut. The number is on his right hand, and his left hand is against the other side of his head. Suddenly, he whacks the right hand against his head and pulls the left hand away — with a number on it that is different from the right. He smiles confidently.)* The number has now passed through my mind, and it is — *(Pulls his left hand down and looks.)* Three! *(Volunteer says no.)* What? That can't be! It went right through my brain! How can anything get garbled going through the brain of Smiling Sam? Impossible! *(He tries again and again, always failing. He even comes up with a zero on one occasion. Finally, he admits defeat.)* All right, maybe my mental magic isn't working too well. But how do I know you didn't cheat? You could have changed the numbers and I never would have known!

Performance Mechanics

Smiling Sam made me think I didn't have to think when I gave a performance: Just be natural and have fun! Ha! Was I ever fooled! There's a lot of careful thought that goes into a performance. The skits in this book give you lots of specific information that helps a lot, but I think I should offer you a few general hints on what to think about and when.

Right now I want to tell you about props. No, not building props, but *setting them up for a skit!* First of all, make sure your props are out of sight (from the audience) until you're to use them. Either keep them in a big box, behind the curtain, or wherever, so they're out of your way, and yet still quickly accessible for when you need them. You don't want to stop the show for five minutes (like you-know-who has done!) while you look for your green and white bowling ball. *"I know I've got it somewhere, folks, and if you'll just wait another minute, I promise you big laughs!"*

Some skits require special setting up, especially if you've got lots of props (like "Open Gizzard Surgery" or "Eating Way Out"). Move quickly and make a few jokes to help pass the time for the audience. Know ahead of time where everything goes. *Practice* setting up.

Remember: Keep props organized, easily accessible, out of sight until needed, and know where to put them for easy use in a skit.

The Monkey You Are!

Props: Another take-anywhere, zero-cash outlay, propless routine!

Comments: If Smiling Sam can turn the world upside-down, Merry Melody can turn kids into animals (although the parents might say that they already *were* animals. You can do the same, especially when working with a nice group of cooperative, bright children.

● ● ● ● ●

Merry Melody: *(Looking curiously at the children)* I didn't know I was going to be clowning around at a zoo! No one told me that! I thought there'd be a whole bunch of children here, but all I see are animals, and funny-looking ones at that! Why, *(Pointing to various children)* there's a gnu, and there's a turtle! *(Pause)* Everybody look up! Way up high, up in the sky! Higher! Stretch those necks! By golly, now I see a whole herd of giraffes! *(Most of the children laugh, but a few want to argue that they are not giraffes or any other kind of animal. MERRY thinks otherwise, though, and does her best to convince the children that they are zoo animals.)* Maybe you're not giraffes, I don't know. I'm just a clown. But I still think you remind me of a strange kind of animal. *(Pretends to change subject.)* TINKER THINKER! Got an idea! How many of you can put your heads between your knees? Like this. *(MERRY MELODY, standing up, bends down and puts her head between her knees. Who can resist the opportunity to do something so ridiculous? Certainly not the children!)*

Ha! Look at that! You look like a whole bunch of ostriches hiding your heads! That's what ostriches do, you know. They hide their heads in things! Ha ha! I told you this was a zoo! *(Pause)* Let's see, what other animals are there? Wow! I see a whole jungle full of monkeys! Every one of you is a monkey! *(Again the children argue. This time* MERRY *is going to have to be a bit more resourceful in convincing them. They're getting wise to her ways.)* Oh, yes you are! Can you scratch your toes with one hand and rub your knee with the other? Go on and try! Look, I can! *(She shows and the children follow.)* And can you scratch your chin and rub your tummy? Can you scratch your tummy and rub your back? Can you scratch your armpit and rub your head? *(The children do as requested and* MERRY MELODY *breaks into laughter. She fooled them into acting like monkeys! She makes fun of them by scratching her own armpit and rubbing her head. Worse yet, she waddles around like a monkey and makes monkey noises.)*

Monkey see, monkey do! Whhooo — whhooo! If you don't look like a bunch of monkeys, it's because you look more like chimpanzees! *(Pause)* What else do I see? I think — no! Yes! I see rabbits! All kinds of rabbits, everywhere! What do you mean you don't believe me? I can prove it to you, plain as the brain in my head — and you can't get much plainer than that! Put your hand on the floor! Put your hand on the table! Here comes that rabbit! Put your hand on your knee! I hear rabbits! Put your hand on your shoulder! Put your hand on your head! *(Points and laughs.)* I gotcha! There's a *hare* beneath your hand, and it's yours!

And some say that Merry Melody has moths in her head, but that's just a matter of opinion. On the other hand, she is a little fluttery at times. . . .

Lie Detector

Props: Nothing less than the most advanced lie-detecting computer in clown technology! Don't hold back when you design this gem. Basically, you only need two light bulbs, sockets, a wooden or cardboard box to attach them to, two switches (so that each bulb can be flashed separately), and an extension cord. To make the contraption look ominous, entertaining and very avant-clownish, slap on lots of bright paint, warning signs, extra wires, nuts and bolts, old television tubes, dials, and anything else that seems appropriate. Have two different signs that can be placed above the light bulbs; one that says "yes" and "no," another that says "true" and "false." Top it all off with a nice, loud horn, and you're ready to detect lies!

Comments: Smiling Sam likes this routine more than any other, for it gives him a perfect chance to interact with his audience — children, teenagers, parents, and grandparents. He also tries to get a lot of different people in the lie detector, so that everyone can feel they've been a part of the action.

• • • • •

(SMILING SAM sets his lie detector on a table and a few chairs on the side. He attaches the "true-false" sign over the bulbs.)

Smiling Sam: Smiling Sam is going to make honest people out of you. I brought along my world-famous LIE DETECTOR and super-computer answering machine. It's guaranteed to work forever, too! No one's ever going to put a fast one over on Smiling Sam! That's what the salesman promised me when I paid a million dollars for this lie detector! Now let's get some volunteers so I can get my money's worth, OK? *(SMILING SAM seats a little boy next to the machine and has him take hold of some wires. The boy's name is "Billy." SMILING SAM assumes the role of a judge/lawyer type.)* Will you please tell the audience your name? *(The boy answers "Billy" and the TRUE bulb flashes on and off.)* Good, you're telling the truth. Remember that I am beginning with simple questions simply to test the machine. Now, have you enjoyed my performance so far? *(Billy answers yes and SMILING SAM leans over to carefully watch the lights. TRUE-TRUE-TRUE!)* You not only told the truth, you told the right truth! Good enough! Tell me, Billy, do you like to play with dolls? *(Billy quickly and unconditionally denies this, but the machine flashes FALSE-FALSE-FALSE! SMILING SAM gets a big kick out of this.)* So you like to play with dolls, do you? Don't deny it, this machine never fails! Ha! I bet you even have a dollhouse! *(Even before Billy has a chance to deny this, the machine flashes TRUE-TRUE-TRUE! SMILING SAM shakes his head.)*

Sorry, Billy. You can get away with lying to your mom and dad, but not to Smiling Sam's lie detector. One more question. We know that you like to play with dolls in your dollhouse, but — see that girl over there? Is she your secret girlfriend? *(Billy says no, he pleads no, but the machine flashes FALSE-FALSE-FALSE! SMILING SAM chuckles.)* That's OK, Billy, everybody lies when it comes to love. You can leave, Billy. I think we've firmly established the type of character you are. And I know just who to interrogate next! *(SMILING SAM cajoles the little girl he pointed to into sitting at the lie detector. Her name is "Jill.")*

So, Jill, you're Billy's secret girlfriend? *(She says no, the machine says FALSE-FALSE-FALSE! Jill is so embarrassed, she's almost the color of SMILING SAM's nose.)* The first question and you're already telling lies! *(Pause)* So Billy and Jill are boyfriend and girlfriend! Are you going to get married and have a bunch of kids? *(She's laughing so hard that she can barely answer no — and the machine flashes FALSE-FALSE-FALSE! SMILING SAM sings.)* Here comes the bride! Here comes the bride! Boy oh boy, what a couple of lovebirdies. I'm sure everybody wants to know why you fell in love with Billy. Isn't that right? *(Audience says yes.)* Be honest, now — is Billy a good kisser? *(She answers no and the lie detector flashes FALSE! SMILING SAM decides she's had about all she can take and calls for new volunteers. This time he gets hold of some grandparents.)*

How are you folks doing today? Having a good time are you? And you think I'm the world's greatest clown, right? *(They answer yes to all of these questions. The machine flashes TRUE-TRUE-TRUE!)* You kids look pretty young to me to be sitting in a clown lie detecting machine. Are you sure your parents know you're here? *(They laugh and the grandfather, deciding to have some fun, says yes. The machine flashes FALSE-FALSE-FALSE!)* Say! You ought to know better than to fib about that! So your folks don't know you're running around town, huh? I could get in trouble having you here, you know. But, I guess it's all right as long as you're married. You are married, aren't you? *(They answer yes and the machine flashes TRUE-TRUE-TRUE! SMILING SAM breathes a sigh of relief, but freezes when a terrible thought enters his mind. He addresses the grandmother.)* And this man is your husband, correct? *(She agrees, but the machine has other ideas. FALSE-FALSE-FALSE! SMILING SAM's mouth drops open and he covers his ears with his hands.)*

That's it! I've had enough of this lie detecting business! This is starting to turn into an X-rated show! *(They sit down [still laughing], and SMILING SAM exchanges the "true-false" sign for the "yes-no.")* We're turning the lie detector into a computer. Instead of asking people — who seem to tell a lot of lies — questions, we'll ask the computer. Computers always tell the whole truth, the complete truth, and nothing but the truth. *(Turning to the computer)* Isn't that right? *(YES-YES-YES!)* That's right. Because you're the world's greatest computer, right? *(YES-YES-YES!)* And, not that I need to ask *(Puffs himself up with pride)*, but you belong to the world's greatest clown, right? *(NO-NO-NO!)* Yeeeaarrrggghh! I don't — it can't — it must be — yes, of course, it's broken! *(Laughing and surprised)* Well I'll be a monkey's uncle! *(YES-YES-YES!)*

DIZZY DUETS

Clownincidence! Merry Melody and Smiling Sam finally do manage to join up. The clown stampede carried them right into the clown corral!

Shootout at the Oh-No Corral

Props: Cowboy hats, six-shooters, holsters, a sheriff's badge, and a long rope.

Comments: Smiling Sam and Merry Melody spent a good deal of time rehearsing the choreography of this routine. You and your partner would be wise to do the same. Try to keep your movements and their timing as identical to your partner's as possible (when called for in the script).

• • • • •

(Sheriff SMILING SAM struts about with a hungry look in his eyes. He pulls his hat down tight on his head, spits on and polishes his badge, and twirls his six-shooter. He's one tough hombre.)

Smiling Sam: I am, as you may have suppositioned, the sheriff of Clowntown. I'm big, I'm tough, and I'm mean. I'm so mean I smile when I say that! *(He flashes a quick smile.)* That's how mean I am. And I'm even meaner today, because I'm looking for a villain, Maleficent Merry Melody! She's been rustling the crops and harvesting the cows! A real perplexing nuisance, believe me! If you see her, I want you to tell me! I'll give you a reward! I've got to go and look for her, but you folks stay here and keep your eyes peeled! *(SMILING SAM saunters off to the left a ways, squats down, and peers into the distance. MERRY MELODY enters from the right, very frightened, and stops in the center of the stage to address the audience. She doesn't see SMILING SAM.)*

Merry Melody: Oh dear! I'm in terrible trouble, and I haven't even done anything wrong! The sheriff thinks I've been rustling the crops and harvesting the cows, but I haven't been! He's wrong, because I know who's really been doing it, and I'd like to help the sheriff find him. Do you believe me? Good! Good! If you want to help me, you've got to be very quiet. You can't even whisper. The only time you can talk is when I ask you a question. Now, I've got to find the sheriff. *(MERRY MELODY creeps to the right, away from the sheriff, and some of the children, despite promises, can't resist telling her where he is. She pretends not to hear and warns them again to keep quiet. After she reaches the far right side, both she and SMILING SAM move backwards toward the center of the stage, stopping when they are inches apart. They each look to their own right, then left, without seeing each other. They circle until SMILING SAM is facing the audience.)*

Smiling Sam: I'm a gonna git that Maleficent Merry Melody if it's the last thing I do! *(They continue their ballet of parallel, silly antics without seeing each other. Finally, after squeezing every last possible laugh from the situation, MERRY MELODY faces the audience.)*

Merry Melody: Have you guys seen the sheriff yet? *(They tell her where he is.)* Ha Ha! How could he be standing right behind me? *I* was just standing there! Now remember . . . shhh! I'll be back. *(Again, MERRY MELODY and SMILING SAM circle and exchange positions.)*

Smiling Sam: Confound! I can't find her! And I'm the good guy and she's the bad gal. Tell me where she is! *(Even though they know better, a few children can't help blurting out that she's right behind him. His eyes go wide, he turns, trips, falls down, and knocks MERRY MELODY over. They both jump up and prepare for a shootout.)* I've been looking for you, Maleficent Merry!

Merry Melody: And I've been looking for you, Sheriff.

Smiling Sam and Merry Melody: *(Together)* I know who's been rustling the crops and harvesting the cows! And it ain't me!

Smiling Sam: *(Surprised)* It ain't? *(Thinks twice.)* Hold it! No more of your tricks. Of course it was you. Who else could it be? I'm afraid I'm a gonna have to shoot you! *(They both pull their guns out of their holsters. MERRY's flies out of her hand. SMILING SAM aims and pulls the trigger, but nothing happens.)* Darn! I

forgot the bullets! And I'm a dum-dum! *(He throws the gun away. MERRY MELODY grabs a rope and makes a lasso with which to catch him. They run in circles.)*

Merry Melody: I wish you'd stop and listen! I'm not the crop rustler! I'm not even the cow harvester! *(They crash into each other as she throws the rope. It slips over them, and before they know it, they're tied together.)*

Smiling Sam: Now you've done it! We're stuck!

Merry Melody: Good! You'll listen to me! I'm not the one you want for committing those crimes.

Smiling Sam: You aren't? Then who is?

Merry Melody: Your mother! That's who!

Smiling Sam: My mother? Dear sweet Mom? Rustling

crops and harvesting cattle? Tsk, tsk! *(A reflective pause)* Come to think of it, she has been acting mighty suspicious lately. She's been complaining that I eat too much! Let's catch her!

Merry Melody: Right now?

Smiling Sam: It's dinnertime! I want her to cook up some of her tasty crops and cattle!

Doctor Golf
and the Teed-Off Patient

Props: Toy golf club, chair, patches, and white cloth strips for mending injuries, and a wad of fake dollar bills.

Comments: FORE!

•••••

(DOCTOR GOLF [a.k.a. Smiling Sam] stands in his office and takes a practice swing with his golf club. He talks to the audience.)

Doctor Golf: Hi! My name's Golf. Doctor Golf. My game is golf. I'm Doctor Golf and I like to golf. I like golf games. Golf clubs. Golf shoes. Golf gloves. Golf balls. Golf hats. Golf lessons. Golf carts. Golf underwear. Golf hamburgers. Golf spinach. I like all those things, but to buy them I need money. I don't have money. I need lots of it. I wish I could figure out how to get lots of money. *(At that moment, MERRY MELODY walks into his office.)* Hello, Merry Melody. How are you?

Merry Melody: I'm great, Doctor Golf, just great! Couldn't feel better. Want to know why? *(He does.)* Because I got paid today! Look at this! *(She pulls out a huge wad of paper money and waves it in front of his nose. He starts sniffing and gets excited. He's got an idea where he's going to get lots of money for golf stuff!)* I'm going to put this money in a bank and get curious. *(DOCTOR GOLF is confused.)* Sure, you put money in the bank and you get interest. See ya later, Doctor Golf! *(She starts to leave, but DOCTOR GOLF moves fast. He grabs her around the waist, picks her up, and carries her to the chair.)*

Doctor Golf: I'm afraid I have bad news for you. I think you're sick. Very sick. So sick you won't be able to make it to the bank. *(To audience)* I'll get her money yet!

101

Merry Melody: But Doctor Golf ! I feel great! I've never felt better! But maybe you're right. A checkup can't hurt, can it? And it certainly can't cost very much money.

Doctor Golf: I'll make you a deal. I'll only charge you if I find something wrong, OK?

Merry Melody: Oh, yes! If you find something dreadfully, dreadfully, DREADFULLY wrong with me, I'd be happy to pay you all the money in the world. *(DOCTOR GOLF smiles big and prepares to examine her. He starts off by smashing her toes with his golf club. MERRY howls.)*

Doctor Golf: As I thought. Bad toe reflexes. Let's hope your knee reflexes are better. *(He smacks her in one knee and then the other. He pulls out some bandages and patches her up.)* Dreadful reflexes of the knee. Darn dreadful. Awful darn. Now stand and touch your toes.

Merry Melody: Are you checking to see if I have stiff muscles in my back?

Doctor Golf: Not your back. Your glutimus maximus! *(WHACK! He hits her on the bottom. [Good thing MERRY MELODY is wearing a piece of cardboard inside her pants!] She screams with pain. DOCTOR GOLF puts a patch on the sore spot.)* Good thing I checked. Dreadful condition.

Merry Melody: *(Rubbing her bottom)* It sure *is* in dreadful condition! *(DOCTOR GOLF twists her arm. When he lets go, it falls limp. While MERRY is gasping with pain, he fashions a sling and puts her arm in it.)*

Doctor Golf: Dreadful. Dreadful anterior appendage ambulatory abilities. Let's hope your head is in better condition.

Merry Melody: Stop! Stop! Don't hit me! I'm sure if you do my head will feel dreadful!

Doctor Golf: Let's be safe and check. Never hurts to check.

Merry Melody: *(Angrily)* Oh yes it does hurt to check! You checked my toes and now they hurt! You checked my knee and now it hurts! You checked my . . . you know what . . . and now it hurts! You checked my arm and now it hurts. I feel simply dreadful! I'm going!

Doctor Golf: Not so fast. We agreed that if I found anything dreadfully wrong with you, you'd be happy to pay me all the money in the world. Hand it over!

Merry Melody: Darn! I do feel dreadful, but . . . oh, all right! But I don't have all the money in the world, just half a million — *(He snatches the wad of money and cackles. MERRY angrily stomps to the other side of the room and stops to think. DOCTOR GOLF hangs on to the money, smiles, and takes a few practice swings.)*

Doctor Golf: Nothing better in the world than a game of golf. Except to have money. Now I can buy golf shoes, golf spinach, golf — YeeoooW! *(DOCTOR GOLF has hurt his back! He's stuck with his arms up in the air, holding the golf club and the money. He's in pain. MERRY MELODY sees his predicament and goes to his side. This time she's the one rubbing her hands and smiling.)*

Merry Melody: What's the problem, Doctor Golf?

Doctor Golf: It's my back. Bad vertebrae. It hurts something dreadful. If you could just kinda twist my shoulders, I'll be better.

Merry Melody: Twist your shoulders? I don't think so. I think what I'll do is get my money back! *(DOCTOR GOLF is mad, but there's nothing he can do to stop MERRY MELODY from taking the money out of his hands. To his surprise, she also takes the golf club.)* And now that I've got my money, I think I'll give *you* a physical examination! Let's start with your glutimus maximus! *(MERRY MELODY begins the exam, displaying nice form on her follow through.)*

SMILING SAM'S SECRETS

Teamwork

For the clown who just wants to have a good, fun time putting on shows, working with a partner can be double the fun. That's not an exaggerated clown fact, either, but the honest truth! When you perform solo, you have fun bringing smiles to the crowd. When you perform with a partner, you can *share* your fun with someone who understands! Not only that, a partner can make the show flow a lot smoother — setting up props, putting them away, doing a solo skit while you take a break and catch your breath (or run to the bathroom!), and offering encouragement when the folks out there aren't laughing.

Of course, having a partner means you both have to set up time to practice together, and you both have to be free at the same time to give shows, and that you get along with each other. A lot of clowns who are concerned about running a clown business find that the added confusion of working with a partner (as well as having to split the fee!) is more trouble than it's worth.

If you're smart, do as I do! Sometimes I work solo, and sometimes I work with Merry Melody as a partner! I have the best of both worlds!

Remember: Partners can be fun and helpful, but they also can add complications (sometimes)!

Telephone Talk

Props: Two play telephones and a trans-stage hookup wire, a party ratchet crank, and a firecracker.

Comments: After getting mangled by Doctor Golf, Merry Melody has developed quite an appetite. Too bad she had to use the telephone to place an order. If you decide to use this routine, you'll earn a place in the hearts of many if you follow up with an informational speech on how to *properly* use the telephone, and how only clowns should do the real clowning around.

• • • • •

(SMILING SAM sits at a table on one side of the stage, looking at his telephone. He is absolutely, positively, bored. Who wouldn't be, looking at a telephone?)

Smiling Sam: I wonder what the heck is the matter with my telephone? It's not as fun as it used to be. When I first got it, it rang all the time! People were always calling up and talking. Boy, did I have a lot of fun! *(sighs)* But, people quit calling. I don't know why. Maybe if I just sit here and concentrate on it, it'll ring! *(SMILING SAM hunkers down and gets serious about his concentrating. By golly, that telephone is going to ring! On the other side of the stage sits another table with another telephone connected to SMILING SAM's by means of a piece of yarn. MERRY MELODY walks up to the table and rubs her stomach.)*

Merry Melody: What was that? I heard something growling. It sounded like a wild rhinoceros. Maybe it — *(Looks down at her stomach)* was my tummy. I guess I'm hungrier than I thought. I haven't eaten anything in weeks. It's not that I don't *want* to eat, it's just that, well — *(She pulls her pockets inside out. Empty. She opens her wallet and sand spills to the floor.)* I'm flat near broke. I don't have enough money to even buy a pizza pie. All I've got is this quarter. Can't buy a pizza pie with a — BRAIN TRAIN! I can't buy a pizza pie,

106

but I sure can *rent* one! I'll call Rent-A-Pizza! Now, where's that number? *(MERRY MELODY searches through her clothing and finds a card with the number. She goes to the phone, starts dialing, and reads from the card.)* Rent-A-Pizza. Low monthly payments, no deposit, easy credit. Call Pizza Pie 3-9 $3/4$-4^2-times the subset of 6r. They sure don't make telephone numbers like they used to. Let me see.... *(MERRY MELODY finishes dialing. SMILING SAM's telephone rings and he jumps up and down, giddy with joy!)*

Smiling Sam: Hot dog! Time for some fun! *(Answers phone.)* Hello! Is that you?

Merry Melody: Of course it's me! Who else would it be? I was dialing Rent-A-Pizza. To whom am I speaking?

Smiling Sam: Sorry, wrong number!

Merry Melody: Oh, I'm terribly sorry. I must have divided the integer by the wrong square root. Good-bye! *(MERRY MELODY hangs up, as does SMILING SAM. SMILING SAM laughs and slaps his knee. This is fun!)*

Smiling Sam: I couldn't have more fun if I paid for it! I always tell 'em "Sorry, wrong number!" and they think they've got the wrong number! But they don't! Because that's my name: "Sorry, wrong number!" Gets 'em every time! Of course, it does hurt the pizza pie rental business!

Merry Melody: I'll just have to try this number again. I'll dial very carefully. I want to rent a pizza pie and I want to rent one now!

Smiling Sam: *(Answering the ringing phone)* Hello!

Merry Melody: Hi — say, didn't I just talk to you?

Smiling Sam: Sorry, wrong number!

Merry Melody: But isn't this Pizza Pie 3-9 $3/4$-4^2-times the subset of 6r?

Smiling Sam: Exactly! A-plus for you! *(Pause)* But, you've got "Sorry, wrong number!"

Merry Melody: You mean you don't rent pizza pies?

Smiling Sam: Certainly! Would you like one for the day or for the week?

Merry Melody: *(To audience)* Whew! I finally got through! Kind of a whacky pizza pie rental place, though. *(To SMILING SAM)* I'll rent by the day.

Smiling Sam: Sorry, we're out of day rental pizza!

Merry Melody: But you just asked if — what kind of outfit is this? Is this a crank number?

Smiling Sam: *(Laughing too hard to hear)* What's that?

Merry Melody: I said, is this some kind of crank number? *(SMILING SAM still can't hear her. In frustration, MERRY MELODY slams the phone down on the table, picks up her party ratchet noisemaker and stomps across the stage to SMILING SAM's side. She "cranks" the ratchet in his ear, causing him excruciating pain.)* That's a crank! *(She walks back to her telephone and speaks to SMILING SAM.)*

Merry Melody: Now, if this isn't a *crank* call, I'd like to rent a pizza pie for —

Smiling Sam: *(Laughing again)* Sorry, we're out of pizza pies!

Merry Melody: I bet you're getting a real bang out of this, aren't you? *(No matter how loud she yells, SMILING SAM can't hear her. Angry, she lights a firecracker and throws it on the floor beside his feet. It explodes and SMILING SAM snaps to attention — for the moment, anyway.)*

Smiling Sam: I guess I am getting a bang out of this!

Merry Melody: I don't care what you get as long as I get my pizza pie! When will you get some in?

Smiling Sam: Never!

Merry Melody: What! Why you — I bet you're getting a kick out of teasing me!

Smiling Sam: A what? *(MERRY MELODY runs across the stage and kicks SMILING SAM in the bottom. Ouch! She runs back to the phone.)* I didn't know I was getting a kick, but I guess I am!

Merry Melody: I'm going to report you to your superiors! What's your name?

Smiling Sam: Sorry, wrong number!

Merry Melody: But how can I have dialed Pizza Pie 3-9 $3/4$-4^2-times the subset of 6r and still have the wrong number?

Smiling Sam: Because my name is "Sorry, wrong number!"

Merry Melody: Why you big telephony! I oughta hang you up!

Smiling Sam: What?

Merry Melody: I oughta — hang you up! *(MERRY MELODY grabs the telephone wire and makes a loop. SMILING SAM sees what she's doing and decides he'd better disconnect. The chase is on!)*

Eating Way Out

Props: All the usual dining utensils and tableware (whether or not they are breakable is up to you and your budget). Also, an old shoe sole, two hamburger buns, a fork with bent prongs, a big spoon with a hole in it, a large bib, a pitcher of water, wind-up snapping teeth, a rubber duck, a rubber snake, rubber spiders, a mop, a fishing pole, a wine bottle labeled "Cold Duck," and anything else you come across that might complement the main course. (Don't forget to include Mom's favorite tablecloth!)

Comments: What clown show is complete without at least one very messy restaurant scene? Certainly not Smiling Sam's and Merry Melody's! And with this skit to guide you, there's no reason you shouldn't have one too. (Unless you're one of those living paradoxes: a neat clown!)

• • • • •

Merry Melody: I never did get to rent a pizza pie. And you know what that means! That's right, I'm a hungry clown! This time I'm going to eat a real meal, and buy it too. I'm going to a restaurant! *(MERRY MELODY sallies over to the nearby restaurant, all one table of it. She's stopped by the waiter, SMILING SAM. He's not your friendliest waiter in the world.)*

Smiling Sam: What do you think you're doing here?

Merry Melody: This is a restaurant, isn't it? I wanted to eat a meal, if you don't mind.

Smiling Sam: Well, I do mind!

Merry Melody: Too bad. My stomach is stronger than your mind, so you'll have to serve me.

Smiling Sam: Oh, yeah? We'll just have to see if your stomach is stronger than my mind. Sit down and I'll serve you. *(MERRY MELODY unwittingly accepts the challenge from SMILING SAM and takes a seat at the table. Just as she sits down, though, he pulls the chair out from under her and she crashes to the floor. MERRY*

110

struggles to get up, grabs the chair, and sits down. She leans forward to put her elbows on the table, but SMILING SAM slides it away. Boom! MERRY reaches out for the table, slides it back, sits down — no chair!)

Merry Melody: What's the big idea? Gimme that chair!

Smiling Sam: Certainly. Will there be anything else?

Merry Melody: Anything else? Yeah, how about a menu! *(He hands her the menu [a large piece of cardboard labeled "Menu"]. But MERRY holds it upside-down!)* What kind of menu is this? Do you call this food? I can't eat food like this, no sirree! *(SMILING SAM turns the menu right side up. MERRY sheepishly accepts the correction.)* That's better. A little. Now what shall I have for dinner? Maybe I'll have the chicken and head-lights special.

Smiling Sam: High beam or low beam?

Merry Melody: Low beam, please. *(SMILING SAM quickly scribbles the order down on his pad. Unfortunately, MERRY changes her mind and he has to tear the order off. Each time she changes her mind, the pile of papers grows — as does the waiter's frustration!)* No, better make that liver and scrub brush. No, how about hot dog and rubber mats? Or should I get hamburger and thumbtacks? Or should I get —

Smiling Sam: You're getting the house special!

Merry Melody: But l don't want —

Smiling Sam: I don't care what you want! I don't have any more order blanks! *(SMILING SAM storms away to place the order. MERRY MELODY seems pleased. The house special! Mmmm, she can almost taste it! But wait — not all is right.)*

Merry Melody: Waiter! Oh waiter! I need some tableware! *(SMILING SAM groans and returns with the tableware. He dumps a dusty, dirty, wadded-up tablecloth on the table. He then hands MERRY a spoon with a hole in it, a fork with badly bent prongs, and a large bib — which he ties tightly around her neck, almost choking her.)*

111

Smiling Sam: There! Need anything else?!

Merry Melody: Well, would it be too much to ask for a glass of water? I always have a glass — *(SMILING SAM moans and shakes his fists and stomps his feet. He turns to get the glass of water.)*

Smiling Sam: What do people expect from me, anyway? Service? Food? Don't they know I'm busy working? *(He returns with a pitcher of water and a glass, which he hands to MERRY MELODY. She holds it up for him to fill. Unfortunately for her, he mumbles and doesn't pay attention. He pours most of the water into her lap. Each time she repositions her glass, he moves the pitcher.)*

Merry Melody: STOP! *(SMILING SAM stops and looks in his pitcher. It's almost empty!)*

Smiling Sam: Why didn't you say something sooner? Water's not cheap, you know, and I can't afford to waste it! *(MERRY MELODY turns her glass upside-down. There's no water for her to drink. She thinks about asking for more, but wisely decides against it.)*

Merry Melody: Uh, do you think I could get my meal? The sooner I eat, the sooner I can get out of here!

Smiling Sam: Good thinking! I won't even cook it! That'll save me some time! *(He brings out a tray of food and sets it on the edge of the table. He announces each item and then tosses it to MERRY MELODY, who struggles to catch it. He gets her hopping from one side to the other. The hamburger is two buns with an old leather sole in between. The spaghetti is a plate of rubber snakes; the appetizers, a plate of rubber spiders; the cold duck champagne, a rubber duck; and the soup, wet. MERRY knows it's wet, because when SMILING SAM announces the soup, he throws the liquid and not the bowl — right into her face!)*

Merry Melody: What's going on here? What kind of service is this? You'd better not be expecting a very big tip!

Smiling Sam: Sorry, but with the house special you just get the soup, not the bowl. Bowl costs extra.

Merry Melody: I don't care how much it costs, bring me some soup *in a bowl*. And right now! *(SMILING SAM sulks off for the soup and MERRY begins eating. Or at least, she tries to eat.)* Mmmm, hamburger. This tastes — yuck! What's this? Part of an old shoe? That may be one hundred percent beef, but it's the wrong one hundred percent. I think I'll try the spaghetti. Blech! What's this? Snake spaghetti! How does he expect me to eat this without paramecium cheese, that's what I want to know! *(SMILING SAM returns with the bowl of soup. He smiles to himself.)* This better be good, or I'm leaving! *(Peering into the soup)* What's that? I hear something. *(SMILING SAM whips out his trusty fishing pole and drops the line into the soup. Secretly, he attaches the hook to a pair of wind-up clacking teeth. MERRY MELODY watches in horror as he hooks something, works it to the top, and pulls out the pair of teeth, rapidly chattering away.)* What are those doing in my soup?

Smiling Sam: Oh, they belonged to Happy Jack. He was the last person who ate here. *(SMILING SAM turns to MERRY MELODY and grins.)* Until you came by. Funny thing, Happy Jack ate the house special too. *(MERRY yells and runs away, frightened that she might end up like the previous customer.)*

Merry Melody: I've lost my appetite! I'm going on a fast, but fast!

Smiling Sam: Wait, don't go away! There's still dessert! We have some delicious cow pies on sale tonight!

MERRY
MELODY'S
MUSINGS

Adapting Performances to Audiences

Guess what I learned when I gave my second performance? And my third and fourth and fifth and every other one after that? I learned that not all audiences are alike! And when the audience is different, your act had better be different too!

When I perform in parades, I only have time for quick, simple gags that I pluck out of my regular skits. When I perform at a backyard birthday party, I'm a lot more relaxed and informal. I try to be more of a fun friend than a PERFORMER. I make up for that when I perform at pizza parlors or banquets or talent shows. That's when I go out of my way to be THE STAR! I'm oh, so theatrical! Of course, sometimes, especially at pizza parlors, I have a chance to quit performing for the entire crowd and "mingle" from table to table so that I can personally and informally perform for different families and groups of people. The rest of the audience likes this because it gives them a chance to quit laughing and eat their pizzas! After I'm done mingling (performing simpler skits like "Baaallooons!," "Magic Act," and "Digital Portrait Drawing"), I go back to the big time, raise my voice, and perform big skits for the whole crowd!

Remember: Adapt your performance style to meet the requirements of performance conditions!

Boxers Who Didn't

Props: Two pairs of boxing gloves, bathrobes, bright, shiny, silky boxing (or jogging) shorts, a pail, a gong-type bell, and a jump rope.

Comments: No eye-gouging! No hitting below the belt! No kidney punches! And especially, no hitting in the face — can't have all that beautiful clown make-up smeared, can we?

● ● ● ● ●

(*MERRY MELODY and SMILING SAM walk on stage wearing their bathrobes and boxing gloves. They act like boxers, dancing about and swinging their fists. SMILING SAM raises his arms to show that he's the champ, and then removes his robe, tossing it on the chair in his "corner.")*

Smiling Sam: I am the CHAMP! I am number one! I am invincible! I cannot be beaten! I am the greatest! I am the greatest boxing clown that ever lived or ever will live! I — *(Chokes. While SMILING SAM chokes on his own words, gasps for air, and sits down on his chair, MERRY MELODY removes her robe, picks up a jump rope, and begins jumping.)*

Merry Melody: He's choking on his own words already, and the fight hasn't even begun! I'm going to be the new champ! I will decimalize my opponent with my digits! I'm going to hit him, hit him, and hit him again! I'm going to knock him to the floor — *(MERRY MELODY trips on her jump rope and falls flat on the floor. Embarrassed, she tosses the jump rope aside.)* Just like this. *(SMILING SAM decides the fight should begin, and strikes the bell. Both boxers jump to the ready, fists held high. SMILING SAM growls and snarls, trying to look as mean and bad as he can. MERRY MELODY isn't what you'd call mean, but she does show spunk. They spar and circle, but never connect.)* Come on, you potato head! You big sissy! You're not so tough! You couldn't squash a fly if you sat on it! Why you're nothing but a big baby that — *(SMILING SAM can't take it any longer. He begins crying! Who says dummies don't have feelings? He howls and sobs and covers his face with his gloves. MERRY is concerned.)* Say, champ, what's the matter? I didn't really mean those things. I was just kidding.

Smiling Sam: So am I! *(SMACK! Sneaky SMILING SAM slugs her! Her guard was down and he wasn't really crying! Talk about strategy! She falls down, unconscious.)* I did it! A first-round knockout! All I've got to do is count to ten and I've won. Let's see — one, two, four, nine, thirteen — no, that's not right. Ten, nine, eight, zero, four and a half, eleventeen — that's not right, either! A,b,c,d,e,f,g,h,i,j,k — darn! I'll never get to ten! *(MERRY MELODY starts to come to. Disappointed, SMILING SAM returns to his corner and rings the bell. He rests while MERRY MELODY struggles to her feet. She's a little dazed.)*

Merry Melody: What happened? Where am I? Did we make it, Sarge? Did we get the bridge? Will I ever eat apple pie again? Tell me I will, please, Sarge, I — Hey! I know what happened! *(She looks accusingly at SMILING SAM, who quickly rings the bell to restart the fight. They start swinging fast and furious. MERRY MELODY shuts her eyes and turns her head. Still, they don't hit each other. SMILING SAM steps back a moment and rests his arms, leaving MERRY to swing. He takes a deep breath before jumping back into the action. MERRY then displays some sneakiosity by kicking SMILING SAM in the shins. He yelps and grabs his leg. While he hops around on one foot, MERRY chases him and kicks him repeatedly in the bottom.)*

Smiling Sam: Ouch! Ooch! Fight fair! Don't kick! At least put some gloves on your feet! *(He can take it no more! He stops, turns, and swings, hitting MERRY in the head. Not really, of course, but that's what the audience thinks. MERRY says "ouch," and returns the punch. SMILING SAM says "oooh!" He swings again, as does she. They quickly develop a quick "Ouch-ooh!" patter, and MERRY again shuts her eyes. SMILING SAM gets tired of exchanging punches and steps back, but MERRY keeps on swinging. They continue saying "ouch-oooh!" until SMILING SAM rings the bell. MERRY opens her eyes and sees that she's been tricked again, and sulks back to her corner. Once again she trips and falls unconscious!! SMILING SAM is alarmed.)*

Oh dear! She knocked herself out! That'll make her the champion! I'd better wake her up! *(He grabs a pail filled with confetti and throws it at her. Unfortunately, he got a little carried away, and the pail sticks to her head! She gets up and staggers blindly, swinging everywhere!)*

Merry Melody: They got me, Sarge, they got me! But I'm not giving up! I'll hold 'em while you and the boys run for it! I'll be OK! Just save some apple pie for me, would you? *(SMILING SAM pulls the pail off her head and rings the bell. She quickly remembers where she is and* *begins boxing.)* I've had it with your sneaky tricks! I'm going to have to stop playing around with you and put you away! Say your prayers, Smiling Sam! *(She bends slightly and begins a furious attack with her arms moving like she was doing the dog paddle across the Atlantic. SMILING SAM defends himself easily, however, by holding one arm straight out against her head. He stands there calmly while she struggles to outstretch his reach.)*

Smiling Sam: I'm getting tired. You wouldn't want to quit, would you? Call it a tie?

Merry Melody: Never! Not on your life! Ha! *(SMILING SAM shrugs and begins slugging it out with MERRY MELODY. Boom — Boom — Boom! After a few punches, their hands connect. When MERRY MELODY pushes in with her right, SMILING SAM pulls back with his left, and vice versa. Before you know it, they're dancing! Having a good time!)* Hey, this is fun! It's better than boxing! It's even better than apple pie!

Smiling Sam: *(Keeping time)* and one — two — three — four — five — six — seven — eight — nine — ten, and one — two — three — four — five — six — seven — eight — nine — ten, and . . .

Lightweight Diet

Props: Wear a shirt that can hold lots of padding. An old long-sleeved undershirt works well. Use old socks and wadded up boxer shorts to simulate muscles in the upper arms and chest. A fake barbell can be made from a broomstick with a plastic milk bottle (painted black) stuck on each end. Each of the bottles should have a small picture hook in them so you can easily attach cards that display the weight. Cards labled "100#" and "200#" should be enough.

Comments: Although Smiling Sam and Merry Melody do some talking in this routine, you can, if you wish, easily perform it in pantomime.

Heave-ho and away we go!

•••••

(SMILING SAM, the heavyweight, is proudly and vainly displaying his huge muscles. His muscles are so big he can hardly walk! Not only that, the muscles [being nothing but old clothes] are a little oddly shaped.)

Smiling Sam: There's nothing more beautiful than a well-muscled clown body! I think I've got more muscles than all the other clowns in the world put together! I may even try out for the Mister Clowniverse Contest! *(He flexes his muscles and continues to strike different poses. Stepping forward, he almost trips over the big barbell.)* Ah! The tool of my trade! The barbell! No, wait, don't embarrass yourselves. I know you're just dying to see me lift the barbell and display my true abilities, but you're afraid to ask a big guy like me to do it. But really, I don't mind. *(SMILING SAM looks down at the barbell and sees that it's labeled "100#." He scratches his head a little uncertainly.)* It's heavy, but I'll give it a try. *(He proceeds to lift the barbell above his head, straining and grunting.)* The hard part is over. I'm through concentrating, so you can applaud anytime. *(The audience finally gets around to applauding, and*

*SMILING SAM sets the barbell down and takes a bow —
pausing only once to flex his muscles. Wouldn't you know
that while he's basking in the limelight, someone comes
by to rain on his parade? None other than skinny, wimpy
MERRY MELODY. She takes one look at his muscles
and her mouth drops open in awe. Then she looks at
her own muscles and tries to flex them. Nothing.)*

Merry Melody: I guess I'm not very strong. Of course, I
haven't practiced at being strong like you have.

Smiling Sam: No better time to begin than right now. Go
on, try and pick it up! *(MERRY MELODY shrugs. What
has she got to lose? She tightens her belt, licks her lips,
spits on her hands, and reaches for the barbell. She gets
a good grip, lifts — BOING! She lifts so high and so
easily she almost loses her balance. SMILING SAM
almost loses his cool too.)*

Merry Melody: Hey! This is a lot easier than I thought!
A little bit of practice goes a long way!

Smiling Sam: Move over! That was beginner's luck, that's
all! *(MERRY MELODY sets the barbell down and
watches as SMILING SAM increases the weight. He*

attaches a label that reads "200#." He squats over the barbell and labors to lift it. It's slow going with lots of grunts and groans and moans, but he eventually holds it high. He then drops it quickly to the ground and wipes his hands, smug in the knowledge that he alone can lift such a heavy weight. MERRY MELODY tries next and — BOING! Nothing to it! She laughs with joy and twirls the barbell like a baton before setting it down.) This is some kind of a trick! I've trained all my life to lift weights, and you — Yikes! *(One more time he increases the weight, this time to "500#." Try as he might, though, he can't begin to budge the barbell. All the yelling and straining in the world won't move it. He falls on his bottom, exhausted. MERRY MELODY moves in and again snatches the barbell as though it were a feather.)*

Merry Melody: I guess you don't need big muscles to be strong, do you?

Smiling Sam: It's a trick! A gimmick! You've got springs in your arms! Magnets!

Merry Melody: I wouldn't do a thing like that, not when it's so easy to pick up. I'll prove it to you. *(MERRY MELODY runs into the audience and grabs a volunteer. She directs her to lift the barbell.)* Snap and curl! Iron and twist! *(The volunteer lifts the barbell with ease. MERRY thanks her and directs her back to her seat. SMILING SAM, now more frightened and shocked than angry, tries again to lift it, but fails.)*

Smiling Sam: All that work for nothing! All these muscles and a lightweight weakling comes along and outlifts me!

Merry Melody: Uplifting, eh?

Smiling Sam: No, it's terrible! Now I feel worthless! All I had was my muscles, and now they're no good! And I've got so many of them I don't know how I'll ever get rid of them all!

Merry Melody: *(Feeling guilty)* Gee, I'm sorry. I didn't know it meant that much to you. If I had known —

Smiling Sam: *(Screaming)* EEEEK! A mouse! A mouse! *(Smiling Sam jumps into MERRY MELODY's arms. He's a little heavier than the barbells, but she manages to hold him for a moment.)*

Merry Melody: Don't worry, a little old mouse won't hurt you, not when — HEY! *(MERRY MELODY lets the big sissy fall to his knees and shake. She looks closely at his muscles and begins investigating. She pokes around and pulls out some old rags.)* Why, you big joker! You don't have any muscles at all! Just rags! You're nothing but a big sissy!

Smiling Sam: Don't hit me! Don't hit me! I might break! *(SMILING SAM begins crying and runs away, vowing to come back with his big brother!)*

Routining

Merry Melody aleady told you about how to set up individual skits, and the importance of having props in the right places at the right times. I'm going to tell you about the importance of having *skits* in the right places at the right times.

My clown shows are all the funniest things you could ever hope to see, from beginning to end (and then some!), but I manage to vary the kind of hilarity from skit to skit. This way my shows don't become monotonously entertaining and rewarding. The practice of variation is known as routining.

I may start out with something low-key and simple, like the "Exploding Balloon" or "Digital Portrait Drawing." Then I'll try something more complex in plot and props; "Photo Fun" or "Unbalancing Water Balloons" fill the bill. I go back and forth from these two kinds of skits to give the audience (and myself!) a little bit of breathing time. I save the real wild skits, things like "Tug of War," for the end of the show so I can end on a high note of excitement.

Remember: For an entertaining, balanced, continually interesting show, vary the types of skits you perform!

Golf Gooforama

Props: Golf clubs and balls, long elastic string, some kind of hole (a cup works fine), pole with a small flag on top, small "sandbox," and a tape measure. Prepare a third golf club so that it can easily be disconnected in the middle. If possible, look for oversized plastic toy clubs and balls in a toy store.

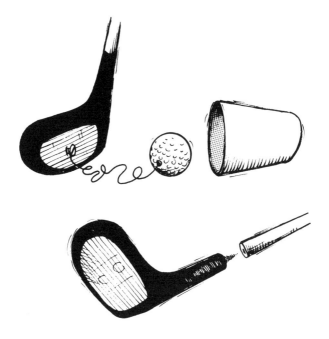

Comments: Keep your feet together, eyes on the ball, and follow through! It's easy! More fun than real golf!

●●●●●

(SMILING SAM walks out with a golf club and golf ball. He takes a big, deep breath of air [coughs slightly], and surveys the green.)

Smiling Sam: Yes inn-deed! It looks like a fine day for a game of golf! This is going to be fun. I've got the whole green all to myself! Well, why waste another moment?

(*SMILING SAM sets his ball down and prepares his swing. His preparation process is quite intriguing, involving, as it does, a lot of bottom wiggling. Every time he gets ready to swing — wiggle, wiggle, wiggle. He finds it annoying and gives himself a slap on the rear.*) Knock it off! I'm trying to concentrate! (*That's better. He aims, pulls back. . . .*) Foooore!

Merry Melody: (*Offstage*) Five! Six! Seven! We shall meet again in a green golf heaven! (*SMILING SAM is flustered by the distraction. MERRY MELODY walks out carrying her own golf club.*) Hi! You don't mind if I join you for a game of golf, do you? I've never played before, and I thought it was high time I learned!

Smiling Sam: It never fails! All right, you can play golf with me. Just make sure you stand behind me and keep quiet. (*MERRY does as instructed — and then some. SMILING SAM re-addresses the ball, pulls back — and MERRY MELODY pulls the bottom of his club off! He swings and misses the ball by a mile. Stunned, he leaves the club where it ended on the follow through, over his shoulder. MERRY MELODY quickly re-attaches the club. SMILING SAM searches the fairway, but can't find the ball.*) Where's my ball? I must have hit it clear out of the park!

Merry Melody: Look between your toes! You never hit it!

Smiling Sam: Impossible! I never miss! Let me try again.

Merry Melody: Sorry, pal. It's my turn! Watch this! (*MERRY puts a ball down and swings. Around and around she goes, and where she stops, nobody knows! When she finally does stop spinning, SMILING SAM is looking in the distance for the ball. MERRY sees that she missed it and secretly picks it up. SMILING SAM is awestruck with her drive. MERRY seems bored.*) Enough of this driving around. Let's put the ball in the hole!

Smiling Sam: You mean *putt* the ball in the hole. Might as well, because I'm sure not going to beat you on the drive. (*MERRY MELODY carefully sets down a cup*

to serve as the hole and returns to SMILING SAM's side.) Ah, yes! Putting! This is where one savors the true sport of golf. All the drama, tension and suspense boils down to this. *(MERRY MELODY hands SMILING SAM a new club. This one is connected to the ball by means of an elastic string. MERRY MELODY displayed the gimmick to the audience while her partner's back was turned, so everyone but he knows what's up. He prepares to putt and MERRY runs over to the hole to hold the flag. He hits the ball straight for the hole! But right as it nears the destination, the elastic string pops it back! SMILING SAM scratches his head. He can't quite figure this out. He tries again and again, each time with the same results.)* Maybe I'm mistaken, but I'd say I'm putting up a pretty steep hill!

Merry Melody: I've never seen a curve ball like that!

Smiling Sam: I give up! I've already got one hundred strokes.

Merry Melody: And every one of them is a strike!

Smiling Sam: I'd like to see you do better! Ha! A beginner who can beat me at putting? Never! *(MERRY MELODY prepares to putt. First, she gets out her tape measure and measures the distance from the ball to the cup. She continually comments with grunts and ah's. She then measures the distance from the hole to SMILING SAM's nose [he's holding the flag at the hole]. She measures anything and everything, including the width of the mouths of some of the audience members.)*

Merry Melody: It's now or never! Wait a minute, maybe it'll be a little later. I almost forgot my sand trap! *(She pulls out an old shoebox filled with sand and sets it down. At the same time, SMILING SAM secretly hands her a new golf ball. This ball is connected by an elastic string to the inside of the cup!)* I can't play without my sand trap! I need the challenge! *(She sets the ball in the box and holds her foot on the taut string. After licking her thumb to check the wind current, she shoots. Zip! Right in the cup! SMILING SAM bends down to investigate, discovers the elastic string, and gets angry. He begins swinging his club at her and chases her all the way to the clubhouse. That's the last time she's invited to the Smiling Sam Invitational!)*

War Is Heck!

Props: Pail for a helmet, toy rifle with rubber bayonet, trash can lid painted red, white, and blue, and a couple of old army coats.

Comments: Although clowns are not morally disposed to making war, they have a lot of fun *thinking* they're great soldiers. Merry Melody and Smiling Sam are no exceptions. Their motto is, "When the going gets tough, get going — the other way."

•••••

Smiling Sam: *(Singing)*
You're in the army now,
You'll never get rich
By scratching an itch,
You're in the army now!
(SMILING SAM is the sergeant and his unlucky recruit is MERRY MELODY. She stands at attention shivering and shaking, for the sarge is one mean clown.) That's right, soldier, you're in the army now. In the army you know your place. Men are men, women are women, and clowns are clowns. You hear me, soldier?

Merry Melody: Yes, sir!

Smiling Sam: What am I calling you soldier for? You're not a soldier — not until I finish training you! And we're not gonna waste any more time talking, either, not when there's a war going on! You see that obstacle course out there? You've got thirty seconds to finish it, starting now!

(This particular clown performance is being held at a large crowded pizza parlor. The place is crawling with kids, babies, tables, pizzas, teen-agers, and parents — and it's all part of the obstacle course. MERRY MELODY takes off, not quite sure how she's going to get through in thirty seconds. The first obstacle is a pack of kids. She announces that she has to straddle them, lines them up on their knees, and walks over them [bumping only a few heads]. She then crawls under a bench and under people's legs! If that's not enough, she — look out! She's walking over the tops of tables, on tables. Move

130

that pizza pie! Hang on to your ice cream! Today's army is on the go! MERRY MELODY finishes and returns to her sarge.)

Merry Melody: Obstacle course completed, sir! Whew, sir, that was a tough one, sir!

Smiling Sam: Too tough for you, I can see! It took you thirty point oh oh one seconds to complete! You'll have to do it again! *(The audience voices its opinion on this decision. People definitely do not want her tromping over their dinners a second time!)*

Merry Melody: I agree, sir! I almost drowned in pizza sauce! It was a nightmare out there!

Smiling Sam: Well, I *am* in a hurry to move on to the next stage of your training. Very well. Here's your helmet and rifle. *(MERRY MELODY dons the helmet [an old pail] and takes the rifle. A rubber bayonet is affixed to the end. She tests the point — ouch! That's sharp!)*

Merry Melody: What do I do with this, sir? Cut the grass?

Smiling Sam: You nincompoop! No! You attack the enemy with it! You poke and you cut, poke and cut, poke and cut!

Merry Melody: Oh, you mean like this, sir? *(MERRY MELODY lunges forward to stab the sarge. He holds his*

hands up and yells, then turns around and bends over. Well, what else is she to do but poke him in the bottom? OUCH! The sarge rubs his sore spot and turns around.)

Smiling Sam: Pretty good, but not quite right. Try again! *(MERRY and the sarge repeat their previous actions.)* Yeee — ouch! That's better. much better! You've almost got the hang of it. One more time. *(This time when she pokes him in the bottom, he yelps and jumps up and down with pain. MERRY beams.)* Perfect, perfect! I couldn't have done better myself.

Merry Melody: I want to try again! *(She lunges forward but the sarge grabs her rifle.)*

Smiling Sam: Take my word for it, you know how to do it perfectly. Time now for a strategy session. If we can train your mind as well as we've trained your physical skills, look out!

Merry Melody: Look out for what, sir? *(He looks at her as though she is the embodiment of stupidity. He takes a precautionary step backward.)*

Smiling Sam: You'll know when you see it — if you live that long. Tell me, soldier, what do you do when you see the enemy advancing?

Merry Melody: Run the other way!

Smiling Sam: Brilliant! Brilliant! You're going to make a fine general one of these days! What strategy, what perception, what — why, you should get a medal for your intelligence! *(MERRY grins from ear to ear as the sarge pulls out the red-white-and-blue trash can lid and straps it around her body.)* This is a very special medal! We give it only to soldiers who are worth protecting — as well as to those who need protecting. Now let's find the enemy and practice our skills! Ah, but if only we could find the enemy! *(MERRY starts shaking and points out at the audience. She can barely speak.)*

Merry Melody: We're — we're — we're surrounded, sir! They're everywhere! *(The sarge throws his hands in the air and surrenders while MERRY runs away. She looks back and sees him. She runs to him [what a brave gal!] and he jumps up on her back for a quick escape.)*

Smiling Sam: Never fear! We shall return! Right after a short break!

Troublesome Children

Shock! Dismay! Immoral Dignation, er, I mean, Moral Indignation! Consternation! United Nations! These are only a few of the emotions I felt when I learned that not all children respond alike to my skits.

There's always *(always)* one kid who doesn't know I'm as funny as I am. She never laughs. She sits by herself and doesn't have friends. She's lonely. When I see one of these, I always make a special point to talk to her, or "volunteer" her into one of my skits.

Then there's the kid who outshouts (can you believe it?) me! He tells everyone my magic secrets. He shouts out my jokes before I can tell them. He knows what surprises are coming up and makes an announcement. He . . . darn him! I always try to spot this kid early and take him aside where I can have a little talk with him. . . .

And every now and then, there's the (excuse my language) obnoxious brat. That brat throws things at me, calls me names, pushes the other kids around, even slugs and kicks *me!* Honest! This is one time I'm not joking! What I'd like to do with the brat is one thing I won't tell. What I *do* do is to try and spot him early and deal with the problem as quickly as I can. Maybe I'll call his parents, or maybe try and make him my friend. If those approaches don't work, I'll grab him almost firmly by the shoulder, stick my big nose right in his face, and try to scare him into behaving. If that doesn't work . . . grin and bear it!

Remember: Spot the troublesome child (or the child with a problem) early and cure the ailment with personal attention!

Clowntown News

Props: Two microphones (doesn't matter if they're real or fake) and two large pads of paper from which to read the news. Also, a two-foot length of wire.

Comments: This is a good routine to use for older audiences. Little kids might not appreciate the subtler parodies or the lack of zany action.

•••••

(MERRY MELODY and SMILING SAM sit side by side at a table with microphones. They're smiling big and wide! When they talk, they use expressions and mannerisms popular with television newscasters.)

Merry Melody: Good evening! I'm Merry Melody —

Smiling Sam: — And I'm Smiling Sam. Together, we're bringing you the news from Clowntown! If you want to know about any funny business, we're your news team. Merry, what's tonight's top story?

Merry Melody: Well, Smiling Sam, it seems we have bad news today from Clowntown. Absolutely no funny business was reported. This is the first time in years such a thing has happened. I'd like to go now to a live interview with the mayor of Clowntown, Laughing Larry. *(MERRY MELODY looks over at SMILING SAM, who is lost in a daydream. She nudges him with her elbow.)* The LIVE INTERIVEW, Smiling Sam, come on!

Smiling Sam: Hmmm? Oh, yeah, almost forgot! *(SMILING SAM runs around to the other side of MERRY MELODY and strikes a very distinguished pose. He's now the mayor of Clowntown, Laughing Larry.)*

Merry Melody: Good to have you with us, Mayor. I'd like to ask you a few questions about today's lack of funny business.

Smiling Sam: Ho ho! What's all the fuss? Ha ha! So what if there was no funny business? It happens from time to time.

Nothing to worry about. Nothing more than a big "media" event, heh heh.

Merry Melody: But Mr. Mayor, isn't it true that today's lack of funny business will hurt your political chances? *(SMILING SAM starts to get angry and shake his fists, but quickly regains control and chuckles.)*

Smiling Sam: I think my administration tried its best. That's what the people will remember. The treasurer tried rolling coins across the floor to the little kids, but it was an uphill battle all the way. The secretary tried making paper airplanes out of the yearly reports, but they just wouldn't fly! The wind was down! The police force tried squirting the citizens with water guns, hoping to make them laugh, but it was already raining. Not one silly, crazy thing happened. I know that's no way to run a government, but that's beyond my control. If only the citizenry would try to tighten up its jaw muscles and laugh a little harder, I'm sure we can come through this mess a funnier, sillier Clowntown! A Clowntown to laugh at! A Clowntown people the world over can make fun of!

Merry Melody: Thank you, Mayor! I'm sure if we just laugh off today's events, everything will work out fine! *(MERRY MELODY turns back to the audience while SMILING SAM runs back to his chair to be the newscaster once more.)* Smiling

Sam, I understand you have the weather for us! I hope it's a little funnier than the news!

Smiling Sam: No worry there! I tell you, this weather just gets crazier and crazier! Early this morning we started out with light snickering in the mountains. In the valleys, of course, as most of you know, we had a general sprinkling of mirth. Joy continued to increase throughout the day, bringing afternoon ripples of chuckles and twinkles.

Merry Melody: That *is* funny weather! I hope these conditions will continue through the weekend?

Smiling Sam: Not only prevail, but improve! I think the valleys can expect frequent guffaws, and in the mountains, there's a chance of thundering laughter!

Merry Melody: I know where I'll be spending my weekend! *(SMILING SAM appears startled by something! He runs to the end of the table and picks up a wire with a piece of paper stuck on the end.)*

Smiling Sam: Yikes! This just came in! Here, Merry, you read it! *(MERRY MELODY takes the note. Ouch! She burns her fingers!)*

Merry Melody: This one's hot off the wire, that's for sure!

Smiling Sam: Read it, Merry! This could be a big bulletin!

Merry Melody: Let's see . . . Mayor of Clowntown, Laughing Larry, reports that things are happily back to normal in Clowntown. All the bureauclowns have shelved important business!

Smiling Sam: Hooray!

Merry Melody: The city employees are playing games instead of working!

Smiling Sam: Ha, ha! Let's make today a holiday!

Merry Melody: And the mayor accidentally ate all the city documents! Oh, it is a good day, Smiling Sam. I'll bet voters won't even reject the new laugh levy!

Smiling Sam: You're right! What are we doing here working? Let's go out and vote for it a couple of times! So long from the Clowntown News Team of Smiling Sam —

Merry Melody: — and Merry Melody! Don't worry, we'll

be right back with live coverage of another funny skit! *(And off they go, hoping to vote four or five times, the way a good citizen should!)*

Clown Crimefighter!

Props: The detective should wear an overcoat, a hat, a moustache, eyeglasses (without lenses is fine!), and carry in his pockets a large magnifying glass, a note pad and pencil, a necklace (preferably a sparkly dime store one), a rubber duck that honks, and a large (4 feet by 4 feet is ideal) checkered or brightly colored handkerchief. The victim of the crime needs nothing special.

Comments: It will be necessary to vary your stage movement from one performance to another. Try to make use of existing furniture and backdrops when "searching for clues." In a pizza parlor, look for clues under tables, on tables, on chairs, etc. If performing in the park or a backyard, make use of trees, bushes, fireplaces, and whatever else comes in handy.

• • • • •

*(Poor MERRY MELODY! She's busy bemoaning her fate!
Her necklace has been stolen and she doesn't know what to do!)*

Merry Melody: Poor, poor me! Someone has stolen my very
favorite necklace! I saw him take it! Now it's gone forever!
Oh, what's this world coming to? *(SMILING SAM dressed
up in his detective garb, happens along the scene. He chuckles
knowingly and speaks to the audience.)*

Smiling Sam: Heh heh! These zippy dames, I tell you. Leave
their necklaces lying around for anyone to pick up. Not too
smart, if you know what I mean! *(SMILING SAM pulls the
necklace out of his pocket and displays it to the audience. He
laughs again and puts it away.)* Say, I've got an idea. Watch
this! *(He turns to MERRY MELODY and changes his tone
of voice. He's pretending to be a real detective! Where does it
all end?)* Oh, ma'am? Excuse me! *(MERRY MELODY turns
and faces SMILING SAM. She's startled and can't say anything.)* I'm the detective assigned to your case by the
Clowntown Police Department. If you don't mind answering
some questions, maybe we can recover your necklace!

Merry Melody: Oh, thank heavens! I thought for a moment
you were the robber!

Smiling Sam: Me? Ha! I'd be a pretty stupid criminal to do
that, wouldn't I? *(SMILING SAM turns to the audience and
secretly points and laughs at MERRY MELODY.)* Now, uh,
if we could get started. Let me get my notebook and pencil . . . there. Tell me, what did this criminal look like?
*(MERRY MELODY looks carefully at SMILING SAM. Some-
thing is on her mind, but she's not talking.)*

Merry Melody: Oh, gosh! I'd say he was about as tall as you are!

Smiling Sam: Well knock me down! Ha! What a coincidence!
Tell me, was he wearing any unusual clothing?

Merry Melody: No, just an old overcoat and a hat. In fact, the
hat and overcoat were identical to yours.

Smiling Sam: The robber must have good taste, that's all I can
say. Let's look for some clues. Maybe some fingerprints, huh?
*(SMILING SAM takes out his magnifying glass and begins
inspecting things. He goes over tables and under chairs*

peering through the lens for a hidden piece of evidence. Failing, he turns to the people in the audience. He searches through the hair of one child.) Nothing but worms in here. Yick! This robber wasn't a worm farmer, was he? *(MERRY says no, and SMILING SAM moves on to someone else's ear.)* I found some carrots in here. The robber didn't leave any carrots behind, did he? *(MERRY again says no, and SMILING SAM gives up looking for evidence. He puts the magnifying glass away and takes out his note pad and begins scribbling down information.)* What else can you tell me about the crook?

Merry Melody: Well, he had a moustache exactly like yours. *(SMILING SAM chuckles and turns to the audience.)*

Smiling Sam: *(To audience)* What did I tell you? She's so stupid she'll never catch on to who I really am! Ha!

Merry Melody: And I think he wore a pair of eyeglasses exactly like yours.

Smiling Sam: How about that? Will wonders never cease?

Merry Melody: He also had a rather large handkerchief that was checkered.

Smiling Sam: *(Pulling out his own handkerchief)* Would I be presumptuous to guess that it was identical to mine?

Merry Melody: Exactly! Of course, he needed a big one because he had an inordinately large nose. Like yours.

Smiling Sam: This is all well and good, but what I'm looking for is something highly unusual, something that would set him apart from the average clown like myself.

Merry Melody: Let me think . . . Yes, I remember now! He carried a rubber duck and squeezed it from time to time.

Smiling Sam: Did it sound anything like this? *(SMILING SAM pulls a rubber duck out of his pocket and squeezes it. It honks a few times.)*

Merry Melody: So close, I'd say the two ducks were hatched in the same nest!

Smiling Sam: It's still not much to base an investigation on, ma'am. Slim pickings. All we know about this crook is that he wore a hat like mine, an overcoat like mine, eyeglasses like mine, was my height, had the same moustache I have, had a large checkered handkerchief like mine, and carried a rubber duck that sounds like the one I carry. *(Sigh)* If only we had something substantial! What was this necklace like? Did it resemble this one? *(SMILING SAM pulls his necklace out of his pocket. MERRY MELODY nods affirmatively.)*

Merry Melody: Remarkable! That necklace is exactly like the one that was stolen. They must have been made by the same jeweler!

Smiling Sam: No doubt, no doubt! *(To audience)* What a dummy! She still hasn't caught on!

Merry Melody: Perhaps if we searched for the necklace . . .

Smiling Sam: Good idea, good idea! Follow me. *(When he turns, MERRY MELODY [who isn't as dumb as SMILING SAM imagined!] snatches the necklace from his pocket without his knowing it.)*

Merry Melody: Hark! I have found my necklace! *(MERRY holds it high for SMILING SAM to see. He's a little perplexed. How could she find the necklace when he had stolen it?)*

Smiling Sam: Yeah . . . how about that . . . ?

Merry Melody: Let's see your necklace again and compare them. *(SMILING SAM reaches in his pocket but comes up empty!)*

Smiling Sam: Hey! It's gone! Someone stole my necklace! *(MERRY smiles and winks knowingly at the audience. She then puts her hand on SMILING SAM's shoulder and leads him Off-stage.)*

Merry Melody: Tell me, did the necklace look anything like mine?

143

Adapting and Modifying Skits

As you probably know by now, the skits Merry Melody and I came up with to put in this book are pretty darn funny! They're also loaded with instructions to give you a fail-safe guarantee of success. Still, I've done enough clowning around in my day to know that changes from the scripted skit are often necessary. Here's what I do when I need to make changes.

Sometimes, like when I do a show in a big auditorium or other big, noisy crowd, I can't talk loud enough for everyone (or anyone) to hear me. That's when my pantomime skills come in handy. I study the scripts and pick out all the *visual* (everyone can at least *see* me) gags. I concentrate on these and maybe add a few extra to help explain the action. I don't use a skit like "Telephone Talk," which consists mostly of verbal gags.

When I work with Merry Melody, I can take a lot of skits I perform solo and adapt them for two clowns. The easiest way to do this is to use Merry for a "helper" instead of a volunteer from the audience. At the very least, Merry can hand me props when I need them, point and laugh at me, and help get the audience excited. When she gets tired of that, I end up working alone for a while.

Being alone isn't so bad, because I can take many two-clown skits and adapt them for use by only one! "Fly Trouble" is an easy skit to adapt, as is "Mopping Up" and "Thank You Kindly." I can perform "Open Gizzard Surgery" by operating on a volunteer from the audience or even on an old mannequin from a clothes store! The mannequin can't make jokes, but the things I pull out of its stomach are sure funny!

Hypnosis

Props: Set of very wiggly fingers, and any convenient, miscellaneous articles.

Comments: A word of warning: Make sure *you* can unhypnotize your partner (if you want to). This is a fun routine that has lots of room for fun and spur-of-the-moment improvisation. Still, it's good to have a few basic ideas going into the routine, which is why Merry Melody and Smiling Sam present them for you!

●●●●●

(MERRY MELODY stretches her arms forward and makes slow, curling motions with her hands and fingers, much the same as Bela Lugosi did in the old Dracula movies. She speaks slowly, hauntingly.)

Merry Melody: Listen one and all! I am the amazing Merry Melody, the hypnotic hypnotist. I can hypnotize anyone, any-

where, anytime, and make them do or say anything I wish! No one is beyond my advanced powers of hypnotism. I will begin with a simple-minded volunteer. *(MERRY MELODY picks out a young volunteer and brings him to the front. She cocks her eyes and continues the waving motions. The boy's name is Kyle. He doesn't giggle too much.)* Watch my hands, Kyle, watch the circles they make. They are making you sleepy, drowsy. Sleepier, sleepier. You're getting drowsy, aren't you?

Kyle: No!

Merry Melody: *(Unfazed)* Yes, you are, you just don't know it. You are getting sleepier. Now! Now you are in my complete powers! Your mind is my slave! You will do as I command! You will wake up only when I snap my fingers! Now, Kyle, I want you to touch your nose! *(KYLE figures he might as well go along with the clown. Who knows, she may be dangerous if crossed! He touches his nose.)* You see! He does exactly as I bid! I am the greatest hypnotist ever! Kyle, you will now go into the audience and kiss every girl! *(Enough is enough! KYLE says no and takes a seat. MERRY is miffed.)*

Some volunteer you were! Somebody must have snapped their fingers, that's all I can figure. I will need another volunteer, someone even more simple-minded than Kyle. But who could possibly be more simple-minded than Kyle? *(Who but SMILING SAM should jump up from a chair in the audience!)*

Smiling Sam: Me! Me! I'm more simple-minded! I'll be hypnotized, please, please! *(There's not much MERRY MELODY can say as SMILING SAM comes running up. She shrugs and begins hypnotizing him.)* Anyway, I don't think you can hypnotize anybody! I think you're a phony! I don't even think you can hypnotize a simple, mindless clown like me. I don't . . . *(SMILING SAM's last words trail off as MERRY MELODY puts him to sleep. He's hypnotized!)*

Merry Melody: You are under my power and will do as I command! You will — *(SMILING SAM starts snoring louder than a speeding locomotive.)* — stop snoring! That's what you'll do! Good. You will only wake up when I snap my fingers.

Now, Smiling Sam, you will tell us your name and your age.

Smiling Sam: *(Droning)* My name is Smiling Samuel Smith, and I'm one hundred and seven years old with the mind of a three-year-old.

Merry Melody: That's no surprise. Tell us, though, who is your secret girlfriend?

Smiling Sam: Benji, the dog. She's real pretty. I'd take her home to dear sweet Mom, but Mom's afraid she'll bring in fleas.

Merry Melody: But Benji is a boy dog! What do you think of that?

Smiling Sam: Oops. Another tragic love affair.

Merry Melody: Who is the last person in the world you would want to kiss?

Smiling Sam: You. Merry Melody, the clown.

Merry Melody: *(To audience)* Whew! What a relief! He's the last person in the world I'd want to kiss me, too. Yick! *(Pause)* Wait a minute though! Let's embarrass Smiling Sam. Let's make him *want* to kiss me. Don't worry, I'll snap my fingers and wake him up before he does. I don't want him to kiss me, I just want him to *want* to kiss me. Smiling Sam, you now want to kiss me more than anything else in the world! Ha! *(Without hesitation, SMILING SAM, still in a trance, gets up and reaches for MERRY MELODY, who jumps out of his arms in the nick of time. SMILING SAM puckers his lips like a giant fish and makes smacking noises. MERRY thinks this is fun!)*

I want everybody to remember what Smiling Sam is trying to do and tell him when he wakes up! He'll never believe it! *(He continues plodding after her. He doesn't move fast, but he's relentless [and kinda weird-looking, too]. MERRY MELODY decides she's had enough.)* All right, I've made a big enough fool out of you. I command you to stop. *(He doesn't.)* Stop! Stop! Oh no! He's not obeying my hypnotism commands! I'd better snap my fingers and wake him up. Wake up! *(Snap)* WAKE UP! *(Snap, snap, snap. Looks like it's going to be a long night.)*
(Turn the page to get a better picture of the situation.)

Open Gizzard Surgery

Props: Fun stuff! A hammer, saw, balloons, big sponge, small bucket of water, piece of rope, shoe sole with a hole, rubber chicken, a papier-mâché or cardboard heart with a clock in the center, a bottle labeled "GLUE," a large cardboard "screen" (18 inches by 36 inches) to hide the surgery from the audience (and to hide the props in), and, if you're one of those fussy, finicky surgeons, a bright, garish barbecue apron.

Comments: Always get a second opinion.

•••••

(Poor MERRY MELODY is down and out. Instead of smiling she's frowning. Instead of laughing she's moaning. With her head hanging low, she walks right into SMILING SAM.)

Merry Melody: Out of my way, clown!

Smiling Sam: *(Concerned)* Hey, Merry Melody! What's the matter with you? You don't look so good.

Merry Melody: That's because I feel bad. I don't feel funny.

Smiling Sam: Oh, no! A clown who doesn't feel funny! That's terrible! *(Pause)* How would you like to feel funny again?

Merry Melody: I'd like to, but I don't see how.

Smiling Sam: I do! You've got a bad gizzard! I'll perform open gizzard surgery on you and you'll be laughing in no time!

Merry Melody: Oh no! Not on me! You're not operating on me! Never! Not a chance! Ha! I wouldn't — *(SMILING SAM hits her on the head with a hammer. She falls into his arms, semiconscious.)*

Smiling Sam: Just a local anesthetic. Sometimes my patients get a little nervous and need something to help them relax. *(He drags her onto the operating table and sets up the screen [MERRY holds it in place] that blocks her torso and the operation from the view of the audience. Her arms, legs, and head are still in view.)* My first patient! I've never operated on anyone before, but I bet it's going to be a lot of fun! Let's see . . . first I need to cut her open! (SMILING SAM takes out a* *big saw and begins cutting. He saws against an old block of wood [that no one sees] for a good loud sound.)*

Ooops! . . . darn! . . . oh, silly me! . . . not again! . . . too far to the right! . . . too far to the left! . . . too far to the middle! . . . I guess we'll have to fix that one in the editing room! . . . There! All finished! *(MERRY MELODY starts to regain consciousness. She lifts her head and stares at her open torso.)*

Merry Melody: Yick! Is that *me?* What have you done? If I stand up I'll spill my beans! I'll — *(SMILING SAM gives her another local anesthetic to quiet her down. Through the operation she watches groggily, occasionally groaning when he removes something.)*

Smiling Sam: That'll keep her quiet. I've got work to do. I'd better check her lungs first. A clown needs to have lungs that pump a lot of hot air! *(He pulls out two balloons, fully inflated. MERRY gasps for air. He examines them closely and decides he'd better cut them in half with his saw. Pop! Pop!)* Weak lungs. That's half of her problem right there! I wonder if that affected her kidneys? *(He yanks out [they're* *in tight!] her kidney — a large sponge soaked with water. SMILING SAM frowns and squeezes the water out — right into MERRY MELODY's face.)* Biggest, wettest kidney I've ever seen! *(Peering intently)* What the heck is this? Wait a minute, I know! It's a spinal cord! *(He unravels the piece of rope and holds it high for inspection. It's filled with knots, including a large slip-knot. He pulls it out to lengthen the cord.)*

No wonder she didn't feel good, all knotted up like that. *(He winds the rope into a small ball and tosses it back into place. But wait! What's this? He pulls out a large shoe sole with a hole in the middle.)* Merry Melody's soul! It's in pretty bad shape too. I'd replace it for her if I only had the right size! I'd better put this back very carefully. *(After putting it back, he jumps with fright! Something is racing around inside of MERRY MELODY! He chases it back and forth and all over. He finally catches it — and holds up a rubber chicken.)* Strange place to keep a pet, but hey, who am I to pass judgment? If that's where she wants it, that's where it'll stay. Say, do you hear that? I hear something ticking! *(SMILING SAM pulls out the old clock with the cardboard valentine heart around it. It's bright red and obviously her heart — obvious to everyone but SMILING SAM. He shakes it and gives it the once-over.)*

153

I don't know why she has this inside of her. It can't even keep the right time! *(He throws the heart away. He then picks up the bottle marked "GLUE" and patches her back together.)* A little glue works wonders. Works better than staples, at any rate. There you go, Merry Melody! All done! Wake up, wake up! *(MERRY MELODY slowly comes to. While she's moaning, SMILING SAM secretly hides all the props and removes the screen. MERRY sits up and rubs her tummy, trying to figure out what happened.)*

Merry Melody: I feel kind of . . . funny!

Smiling Sam: Great! That's how a clown should feel. Funny! Ha! The operation was a success! I removed your old ticker, squeezed your kidney, unraveled your spinal cord, popped your lungs, and glued you back together! But I did leave in the chicken!

Merry Melody: A chicken! I had a chicken in me? Oh, I knew I shouldn't have eaten those scrambled eggs! I — hey! How'd you get all those things out of me? You didn't operate on me, did you? *(He nods.)* No wonder I feel funny! And if it's the last thing I do, you're going to feel even funnier! *(She picks up the hammer and starts chasing SMILING SAM, vowing to give him local anesthetics in every one of his locales.)*

154

Safety First!

Clowns are entertainers, not daredevils! And audience members should be spectators, not victims! Play it super safe at all times. Don't use firecrackers (as in the "Clown Camera") unless you're absolutely sure of what you're doing and even more sure that no one will be in danger. (Make sure they're legal in your city or state, too.) Be careful when dealing with any kind of flame (candles, matches, flash paper), especially when performing indoors.

Likewise, be careful of falling props. Juggling can be dangerous, especially in crowded places. Lifting things above your head (as in "Unbalancing Water Balloons") should be done with caution. When throwing or swinging things (like golf clubs or baseball bats), DON'T lose your grip!

Sometimes clowns can't help performing in VERY crowded conditions, but when possible, make sure the squirrely little kids are safely away from your performance area. Kids have a way of sneaking up on you and crawling between your toes.

Also, make sure your props are in good condition. No sharp edges or loose pieces that might fly off. Keep kids out of your prop storage area — you don't want any firecracker or flash paper falling into the wrong hands!

Remember: Safety is funny, danger is dumb.

Mopping Up

Props: Four buckets, a mop, water, and lots of confetti.

Comments: This is an old classic routine that can be performed as successfully in pantomime as with dialog. On hot days, in outdoor performances, with a *very* friendly crowd, Merry Melody suggests that you actually throw one bucket of water into the audience. (She'll do anything for attention!)

•••••

(MERRY MELODY is hard at work, surrounded by buckets of water, scrubbing furiously with mop. She's scrubbing furiously because she is furious!)

Merry Melody: What a life! All I do, all day long, is clean up after people! Why can't people be clean and neat like I am? Especially — mmm — especially that Smiling Sam. *(While she scrubs away, who should walk in but SMILING SAM? MERRY MELODY doesn't see him, so he sneaks up behind her. She stops to rest and leans on her mop. When she does, he pulls it away and she falls down with a CRASH!)*

Smiling Sam: Ha ha! You don't look like you're working very hard, Merry Melody, not when you lie down! Here, get back to work! *(He plops the mop in her face and turns away laughing. MERRY MELODY isn't laughing, though. She's more furious than ever! She gets up and starts mopping again.)*

Merry Melody: He makes me so mad! I'd like to use his head to mop these floors!

Smiling Sam: Quit talking on the job! You don't get paid to talk! *(SMILING SAM emphasizes the point by kicking her in the bottom.)*

Merry Melody: That does it! You've gone one foot too far with me, Smiling Sam!

Smiling Sam: Oh yeah? *(Laughing)* I'm ascared! I'm ascared! Ha! What can you do about it? You just work here!

Merry Melody: I can do this! *(She lifts her mop and swings at his head — he bends down in the nick of time. She swings at his legs and he jumps up, narrowly avoiding being hit.)*

Smiling Sam: Ha! You can't even hit me with a mop! *(He starts laughing so hard he doesn't see her take another swing. BOOM! Right in his face! She holds the mop so the strings hang down over his eyes. Darn him anyway, he just laughs!)* Ha! Thanks for reminding me that I need a haircut! *(He pulls the strings back over his head, trying to style his new hairdo. MERRY snatches the mop away and tosses it on the floor.)*

Merry Melody: How about a shampoo to go with it?

Smiling Sam: A shampoo! Ha! What a joker you — YIKES! *(SMILING SAM sees MERRY pick up one of her buckets and march toward him. He backs slowly away.)* Now wait a minute, Merry, you don't want to do that.

Merry Melody: Oh, yes I do!

Smiling Sam: Oh, no you don't! What'll you use to clean the floor with? Ha ha! *(She throws the water from the bucket at him — but that sneaky guy ducks just in time.)* Ha ha! You're lucky to hit the floor!

Merry Melody: I'm lucky I've got three more buckets of wet, slimy, dirty mop water is what I am! *(She grabs a second bucket and goes chasing after SMILING SAM. Back and forth they go, SMILING SAM continually taunting MERRY, and MERRY always trying to get the best possible shot. She finally throws the water — and misses again!)*

Smiling Sam: Maybe I'd better get my bathing suit! This place is filling up with water, and the only way I'll ever get wet is to go swimming! Come on, Merry Melody, try again! *(MERRY gets the third bucket and gives chase. This time SMILING SAM runs in front of the audience. In less than one half of a second people figure out that if MERRY throws the water [with her poor aim], they'll be the ones who get soaked. MERRY starts to throw it a half dozen times, but always holds back at the last second. Eventually, SMILING SAM works away from the audience. MERRY throws and — SPLASH! The water hits SMILING SAM straight on!)*

Ha! Beginners luck! And it was only a drop of water! My whole backside is still dry! You couldn't hit me again in a million years!

Merry Melody: Oh, yeah? Watch this! *(She gets the fourth bucket, which is, unbeknownst to the audience, filled with*

158

confetti, not water. Not giving anyone time to think, he runs into the audience. MERRY doesn't waste time either — she throws the confetti! Everyone screams and thinks they're wet — until they try to dry off. MERRY takes some more confetti out of her pockets and refills the bucket. She throws the "water" at SMILING SAM several more times, making sure just about everyone in the audience has the opportunity to get soaked. Finally, she chases him back onto the stage where he picks up the buckets and mops and runs away.)

School's Out!

Props: A chair, giant-sized rubber bands, a few pieces of paper, yardstick, chair, blackboard, and a shaving cream pie.

Comments: Merry Melody continually strives to enlighten Smiling Sam. If only he put the same effort into his studies that he puts into his pranks! If you happen to perform at any school functions, this routine will win the hearts of the kids — and lose the trust of the teachers.

• • • • •

(SMILING SAM sits in his chair, fidgeting and fussing. MERRY MELODY points to the blackboard with her yardstick. She's written "FINAL EXAM.")

Merry Melody: You'd better pay attention, Smiling Sam. Today is your final exam, and if you don't pass, you won't be properly prepared for adulthood!

Smiling Sam: But I don't want to be in adulthood! I want to be a clown! Clowns have all the fun!

Merry Melody: I don't care what you want. The school knows what's best for you! Now . . . *(She turns to the blackboard, erases it, and writes "LATIN." Meanwhile, SMILING SAM makes a paper airplane and flies it. MERRY MELODY sees it out of the corner of her eye.)* You'll get a swat for that, Smiling Sam! *(Raises yardstick.)*

Smiling Sam: But teacher, I didn't do it! Honest! He did it! Give him the swat! *(SMILING SAM points to a guilty-looking boy in the audience. MERRY advances on him, slapping her yardstick in her hand.)*

Merry Melody: Is that true, young man? Did you throw that airplane? Am I going to have to give you a swat? *(The poor boy, not really sure if she'd actually swat him [but laughing nonetheless], says SMILING SAM threw it. MERRY shakes her head.)* I don't know who to believe. If it happens again, though, you're *both* going to get swats! Is that understood? Good. Now, Smiling Sam, it's time for your

Latin test. Are you ready? You may begin.

Smiling Sam: Adulthood fax pax. Potatus mish mash. Merray Melodium non teachumus. Smilingual Samuel est clowni supremus! Et cetera, et cetera, ipso facto!

Merry Melody: Wonderful. Excellent! I don't have the faintest idea what you said, but it sure sounded good, and that's all that counts in adulthood. I knew you'd pass! My eye doctor said I had good students. He said he'd never seen such fine pupils! *(MERRY turns to the audience and bats her eyes. Meanwhile, SMILING SAM throws a rubber chicken at her. Controlling her temper, she picks it up and points to the blackboard. She writes "GEOMETRY.")*

I'll overlook the throwing of this chicken if you can tell me what you know about geometry. Can you use it in everyday life?

Smiling Sam: First of all, *I* didn't throw the chicken, *he* did! Second of all, I cannot only use geometry in everyday life, I can use it in a sentence. *(Pause)* One day a little acorn fell into the ground where it began to grow. It grew and grew until finally it said, "Gee, I'm a tree!"

Merry Melody: Excellent! You're already smarter than most adults! *(She turns and writes "PHYSICS" on the blackboard. How can SMILING SAM resist shooting one of his giant rubber bands at her? It hits and she yelps. She goes immediately to the guilty-looking boy in the audience and shakes her stick at him.)* One more time, young man, and you'll go to the principal's office. Keep it up and you'll spend your life in prison! *(Turns to SMILING SAM.)* Tell me about physics!

Smiling Sam: Teacher, I've prepared a special experiment for physics. And you can help! Just stand on my chair, shut your eyes, bend *waaay* over — good! Now, I take your yardstick and swing from fulcrum point *a* with *b* number of foot pounds at *c* speed, connecting here at *(Points to her bottom)* location *x*, causing you to receive the foot pounds and fly to point *f*. Let me show you! *(SMILING SAM whacks her on location x. An uncalculated by-product of the formula is her scream of one hundred decibels! She rubs her bottom and slowly walks to the blackboard. She picks up the rubber chicken.)*

Merry Melody: You know your physics, all right. But what do you know about cooking? *(SMILING SAM shouts with glee and throws a pie in her face!)*

Smiling Sam: That's what I know about cooking! Clown cooking, that is! I don't want to know nothing about adulthood because I'm a clown and that's that!

Merry Melody: *(Angrily)* Your only problem, Smiling Sam, is that I'm a better clown than you are! *(She picks up her yardstick and gives chase! Somewhere in all of this, there's a lesson to be learned — maybe.)*

On Being a Clown

It's true! Clowns have more fun!

Clowns make people happy. They make little kids happy, adults happy, and grandparents happy. They can get away with the Cuh-Raziest things!

A smart clown keeps himself or herself happy and interested in clowning by being eager and enthusiastic to learn new things, try new skits, and teach others how to clown around. A smart clown never grows overconfident or prideful with his accomplishments, for if he does, that magic part of him starts withering up. Audiences sense that when it happens, believe me. You can fool yourself but not the audience.

A clown should always be neat, clean, and courteous, not only when performing, but when doing clown business (making arrangements for performances, meeting people on the street who remember you as a clown, etc.). Good clowns don't expect an audience to meet their demands. They're there to meet the *audience's demands!* Good clowns never speak negatively about their experiences with particular audiences or sponsors, nor do good clowns put down other entertainers (especially other clowns!).

Remember: A good clown is always a fun, friendly person!

Fly Trouble!

Props: Two BIG flyswatters. You can make your own or, better still, buy some professional quality ones from your prop supplier.

Comments: Actually, Smiling Sam's and Merry Melody's antics aren't that much different from what anyone else goes through in trying to swat the elusive fly. What makes them (and you!) entertaining to watch is their unique display of *style.*

● ● ● ● ●

Merry Melody: Life couldn't be better, could it, Smiling Sam?

Smiling Sam: For once, I agree with you! It's a beautiful day! Warm, sunny . . . ahhh! I think I'll just stretch back and take a nap! *(They both lie down and close their eyes, sighing with satisfaction. All is well, except — except for something itching SMILING SAM's nose. A fly! He brushes at it again and again. It leaves him and goes to MERRY MELODY's nose. She sends it back to SMILING SAM, who is now quite perturbed. He jumps to his feet, followed by MERRY MELODY.)* It's that darn fly! Every summer he bothers me!

Merry Melody: I bet it's the same one that bothers me too! *(They search the air for the fly. Their eyes dart about. Their heads twist and turn. Their bodies bend. Smack! They crash into each other.)*

Smiling Sam: Ouch! We'd better be careful!

Merry Melody: What we'd better do is *swat* that fly, and *swat* him fast! This is a nice day and I want to enjoy it.

Smiling Sam: Let's get our flyswatters! *(MERRY MELODY nods her head in agreement. In a moment, they're each holding a giant, humongous flyswatter.)*

Merry Melody: If these don't get him, nothing will! *(They jump into action, eyes peeled, flyswatters poised. MERRY takes a few quick swings and misses, as does SMILING SAM.)*

Smiling Sam: Don't worry, we'll get him! Our brains are

bigger than the brains of a fly. *(MERRY looks at him as though she's not quite sure she agrees.)* Well, maybe not. But if we put 'em together they'd be bigger! *(The fly starts circling MERRY. She tries chasing it and gets dizzy. Finally, her balance almost gone, she stops and accidentally drops the flyswatter. When she bends over to pick it up, SMILING SAM sees the fly on her bottom.)* FREEZE! Don't move an inch! I got him right in my sights, and if you move, he'll fly away. *(SMILING SAM hauls off and swings with all his might! Whack! MERRY yelps and jumps forward, doing a somersault.)*

Merry Melody: Did you get him?

Smiling Sam: You bet I did! Right on the — *(They see the fly buzz back.)* Oops! I thought I had him! Every year I think I swat him, but he always comes back! *(The fly flies between them as they face each other. MERRY watches him land on SMILING SAM's head.)*

Merry Melody: Hold still! He's on your head! *(MERRY swings her flyswatter down on his head — and misses. The fly buzzes to MERRY's head. SMILING SAM tries his luck and fails. The fly goes back and forth from head to head — as do the flyswatters. Finally, after knocking themselves silly,* *they step back and try to regain their composure.)* I see him! He's coming straight at me! *(She gets ready to swing at the fly like a batter hitting a baseball. The fly crosses the plate, she swings —)*

Smiling Sam: *Steeerike* one! *(Again the fly comes.)* Steeerike two! *(And again!)* It's a hit! A fly into center field! *(SMILING SAM backs up to catch it. He looks up, eyes open — and mouth open.)* I got it! I got it! *(They follow the fly down. Plop! SMILING SAM snaps his mouth shut and gulps.)*

Merry Melody: Did you catch him? I don't see him on the flyswatter.

Smiling Sam: I caught him all right. In my stomach! *(SMILING SAM starts twitching around as though being propelled from within by a very strong force. The fly is still alive! MERRY MELODY doesn't waste time before she starts swatting SMILING SAM.)*

Merry Melody: You hold him while I swat him! We'll get that fly! One way or another, we're going to have fun today!

Thank You Kindly

Props: A large sketch pad.

Comments: Sooner or later, all good things must come to an end. Your performance is no exception. To make sure you're invited back again, do like Merry Melody and Smiling Sam: Let your audience know you appreciated them as much as they appreciated you.

•••••

(MERRY MELODY is facing the audience, trying to draw something on her large sketch pad. She looks carefully at the audience, squinting her eyes, holding her thumb up for perspective, trying in vain to find a certain something. She's having some problems and stops to scratch her head. Along comes SMILING SAM.)

Smiling Sam: Hello, Merry Melody. What are you working on?

Merry Melody: Hi, Smiling Sam. I'm just trying to make a drawing here, but I can't seem to get a handle on it. *(SMILING SAM looks at it and laughs. MERRY gives him a look of warning and the smile vanishes to be replaced with a look of genuine concern. He examines the drawing more closely, comparing it occasionally to the audience.)*

Smiling Sam: What exactly are you trying to say with this drawing?

Merry Melody: *(Very much the artist)* Well, like, you know, I'm trying to express my innermost feelings, hoping to trans-clownify the futility of using a two-dimensional medium in combination with the mind. You dig, daddy-o?

Smiling Sam: I gave up digging to be a clown.

Merry Melody: Then let me put it like this: I want to let everybody know how much fun we had today, and how nice they were to us, and how we can't wait to come back again!

Smiling Sam: That's easy! *(He takes a pencil and draws on the pad.)* Just make a line right here, a circle there, create a

167

little more depth here, and voilà! You've said it! *(MERRY MELODY's eyes go wide with joy. She takes the pad and turns it to face the audience. It reads "THANKS!" They take a bow and exit for the last time, remarkably, without trying to hurt or chase each other.)*

Clowntown turned out to be a pretty fun place, didn't it?

Appendix

Organizations

Clowns of America
2715 E. Fayette St.
Baltimore, MD 21224

Clowns of America (COA) boasts over 10,000 members, features a monthly magazine, *Calliope,* and sponsors regional and national conventions. Don't let another minute pass before writing to COA for more information!

Filmstrips

From Contemporary Drama Service, Box 7710, Colorado Springs, CO 80933

Be a Clown: An Introduction to the Art of Clowning
by Main Stage Productions

Clowning for Kids
by Ted Zapel

Whiteface Clown Make-up
by Dana Nye

Skits and Plays

From Contemporary Drama Service, Box 7710, Colorado Springs, CO 80933

Clown Hits and Skits
by Richard Strelak and
Marty Sherman
20 skits. Includes booklet, "How to Write Your Own Clown Skits"

The Clown's Balloons and Other Mime Sketches
by Daniel Robb and
Michael Sturko. 5 skits.

Here Come the Clowns
by Clarice Moon
20 skits.

Publications

LaughMakers
108 Berwyn Ave.
Syracuse, NY 13210

A bi-monthly magazine which covers the whole field of light-hearted entertainment. Includes several monthly columns on clowning by people such as Leslie Homann, Marcia Graham, and Steve Rancatore.

The Clown Connection
20 Richmond Street
Dover, NH 03820

Books

Bishop, George. *The World of Clowns* Los Angeles: Brooke House Publishers, 1976.

Carlo. *The Juggling Book.* Random House, New York, 1974

Hartisch, Karl, "Whitey." *Introduction to Clowning* Available through Clowns of America, P.O. Box 30, Eaglesville, PA 19408.
This book covers all aspects of clowning — characters, costuming, clown gestures, acting, ethics and rules of behavior.

Hugill, Beryl. *Bring on the Clowns* Secaucus, NJ Chartwell Books, Inc., 1980.

Kerns, Ernie. *How to Be a Magic Clown.* 2 vols. Magic, Inc. Chicago, 1960, 1968.

Kipnis, Claude. *The Mime Book* Meriwether Publishing Ltd., 1988.

Liebig, Ernie and Jean. *Clowning Is —* Bullard, TX Happy Enterprises, 1980.

McVicar, Wes. *Clown Act Omnibus* Meriwether Publishing Ltd., 1986 Available from Contemporary Drama Service, Box 7710, Colorado Springs, CO 80933 Includes over 200 workable clown acts.

Meyer, Charles R. *How to Be a Clown* David McKay Co. New York, 1977.

Sanders, Toby. *How to Be a Complete Clown* Stein and Day New York, 1978.

Speaight, George. *The Book of Clowns* New York MacMillan Publishing Co., Inc., 1980.

Stolzenberg, Mark. *The Clown for Circus and Stage* Sterling Publishing Co. New York, 1981.

Swortzell, Lowell. *Here Come the Clowns* New York The Viking Press, 1978.

Towsen, John H. *Clowns* Hawthorn Books Inc. New York, 1976.

Wiley, Jack. *Basic Circus Skills* Stackpole Books Harrisburg, PA, 1974

ABOUT THE AUTHOR

A fondness for juggling led Happy Jack Feder into many years of clowning. He also has performed as a mime and puppeteer. His varied experiences became the basis for CLOWN SKITS FOR EVERYONE and MIME TIME. He lives with his wife and four-year-old daughter, Zu Zu (a budding juggler), in Montana, where he is owner/operator of Happy Jack's Bakery and a literature student at the University of Montana.

ABOUT THE ILLUSTRATOR

Lafe Locke has been a freelance cartoonist for many years. His cartoons have appeared in more than 60 publications and in educational filmstrips, books, and posters. He has been the editorial cartoonist for the MAINE SUNDAY TELEGRAM for the past 16 years. His past occupations include newspaper reporter, magazine editor, and creative director at several advertising agencies. He lives with his wife on an island off the coast of Maine.

NOTES

NOTES

NOTES

NOTES

ORDER FORM

MERIWETHER PUBLISHING LTD.
P.O. BOX 7710
COLORADO SPRINGS, CO 80933
TELEPHONE: (719) 594-4422

Please send me the following books:

_____**Clown Skits for Everyone #TT-B147**　　　**$9.95**
by **Happy Jack Feder**
A delightful guide to becoming a performing clown

_____**Clown Act Omnibus #TT-B118**　　　**$9.95**
by **Wes McVicar**
Everything you need to know about clowning

_____**The Mime Book #TT-B124**　　　**$10.95**
by **Claude Kipnis**
A comprehensive guide to the art of mime

_____**Learning With Puppets #TT-B136**　　　**$6.95**
by **Hans and Karl Schmidt**
An illustrated guide to making puppets in the classroom

_____**Send In His Clowns #TT-B190**　　　**$7.95**
by **Stephen P. Perrone and James P. Spata**
A workshop manual for training clown ministers

_____**The Clown Ministry Handbook #TT-B163**　　　**$8.95**
by **Janet Litherland**
The first and most complete text on the art of clown ministry

I understand that I may return any book
for a full refund if not satisfied.

NAME: _____

ORGANIZATION NAME: _____

ADDRESS: _____

CITY: _____ STATE: _____ ZIP: _____

PHONE: _____

☐ **Check Enclosed**
☐ **Visa or Master Card #**_____

Signature: _____
(required for Visa/Mastercard orders)

COLORADO RESIDENTS: Please add 3% sales tax.
SHIPPING: Include $1.50 for the first book and 50¢ for each additional book ordered.

☐ *Please send me a copy of your complete catalog of books or plays.*

ORDER FORM

MERIWETHER PUBLISHING LTD.
P.O. BOX 7710
COLORADO SPRINGS, CO 80933
TELEPHONE: (719) 594-4422

Please send me the following books:

_____**Clown Skits for Everyone #TT-B147** $9.95
by Happy Jack Feder
A delightful guide to becoming a performing clown

_____**Clown Act Omnibus #TT-B118** $9.95
by Wes McVicar
Everything you need to know about clowning

_____**The Mime Book #TT-B124** $10.95
by Claude Kipnis
A comprehensive guide to the art of mime

_____**Learning With Puppets #TT-B136** $6.95
by Hans and Karl Schmidt
An illustrated guide to making puppets in the classroom

_____**Send In His Clowns #TT-B190** $7.95
by Stephen P. Perrone and James P. Spata
A workshop manual for training clown ministers

_____**The Clown Ministry Handbook #TT-B163** $8.95
by Janet Litherland
The first and most complete text on the art of clown ministry

*I understand that I may return any book
for a full refund if not satisfied.*

NAME: _____

ORGANIZATION NAME: _____

ADDRESS: _____

CITY: _____ STATE: _____ ZIP: _____

PHONE: _____

☐ **Check Enclosed**
☐ **Visa or Master Card #**_____

Signature: _____
(required for Visa/Mastercard orders)

COLORADO RESIDENTS: Please add 3% sales tax.
SHIPPING: Include $1.50 for the first book and 50¢ for each additional book ordered.

☐ *Please send me a copy of your complete catalog of books or plays.*